MUSIC BEFORE THE CLASSIC ERA

MUSIC BEFORE THE CLASSIC ERA

An Introductory Guide

BY

R. STEVENSON

GREENWOOD PRESS, PUBLISHERS
WESTPORT, CONNECTICUT

Library of Congress Cataloging in Publication Data

Stevenson, Robert Murrell.
    Music before the classic era.

    Reprint of the 1958 ed. published by Macmillan,
London.
    "Musical examples" p.
    Bibliography: p.
    1. Music--History and criticism.   I. Title.
ML160.S85 1973   780'.9   73-9131
ISBN 0-8371-6986-0

This edition originally published in 1958 by Macmillan & Co.
Ltd., London

Reprinted with the permission of St. Martin's Press.

Reprinted in 1973 by Greenwood Press, Inc.
51 Riverside Avenue, Westport, CT 06880

Library of Congress catalog card number 73-9131
ISBN 0-8371-6986-0

Printed in the United States of America

10 9 8 7 6 5 4 3 2

PREFACE

THE time-span covered in this introduction to pre-Classic music extends from Biblical antiquity to approximately the middle of the eighteenth century. In order to limit the subject, only theories of music and examples of musical literature which possibly may interest the general reader have been chosen for treatment. Since the author's purpose is merely propaedeutic, no attempt has been made at an encyclopaedic thoroughness nor at an allotment of space in exact proportion to a composer's historical importance.

The author's sincerest thanks are due to Dr. H. K. Andrews of New College, Oxford, to Mr. Bernard W. G. Rose of Queen's College, Oxford, and in particular to Professor J. A. Westrup of the Oxford University Faculty of Music, for invaluable counsel and guidance during the time this Introduction was being written. The sole responsibility, however, for style, presentation, and facts, lies with the author. Miss Mary Neighbour of Oxford did valiant service in preparing the typescript, and the author is also indebted to his publishers for many helpful suggestions.

R.S.

QUEEN'S COLLEGE, OXFORD
December, 1954

CONTENTS

LIST OF MUSICAL EXAMPLES

viii

CHAPTER I

THE MUSIC OF ANTIQUITY

Three main methods have been used in studying ancient music. The first has involved a search for surviving examples preserved either in written form or in oral tradition. The second has involved a study of archaeological instruments which the Egyptians, Assyrians, or Greeks may have used. The third has involved the collection of musical references occurring in such ancient writings as the Bible, the Talmud, and the works of Plato, Aristotle, Aristoxenus, Euclid, Athenaeus, Ptolemy, and Aristides Quintilianus.

The first method has been almost barren of result as far as Hebrew music is concerned. The ancient Hebrews do not seem to have developed any way of writing down their music, and none of it has survived in oral tradition with the exception perhaps of certain ritual melodies still preserved among the isolated Yemenite Jews living in South Arabia. The ancient Greeks, on the other hand, did practise a system of musical notation, and a few scattered examples of their written music survive.

The second method, involving the study of archaeological instruments, has on the contrary been found rather fruitful. Clues to the actual shape, size, and way of playing of ancient instruments have been discovered in the literature of antiquity. Still more valuable for study purposes, however, has been the reconstruction of ancient instruments in facsimile of those found in reopened tombs or in other remains that have lain undisturbed for centuries. Representations of ancient instruments on pottery, in

I

murals, in bas-reliefs, and in pieces of statuary have also proved useful.

One of the principal musical scholars of the nineteenth century, F. J. Fétis (1784–1871), based his essay concerning Egyptian music almost entirely on archaeological evidence recovered from reopened tombs in the Nile valley. At the museum in Florence which Fétis persuaded Verdi to visit when the latter was writing his Egyptian opera, *Aida*, was preserved an ancient Egyptian flute enthusiastically described by Fétis as an open sesame to the Egyptian musical system. In our own century Kathleen Schlesinger has constructed a wind-instrument in imitation of the ancient *aulos* which she has described as a key to the understanding of Greek scale-systems. Another investigator of ancient music in our century who has appealed to the testimony of archaeological instruments, or those constructed in imitation of them, has been F. W. Galpin in his book, *The Music of the Sumerians and Babylonians*.

The third method of studying ancient music, the collection and interpretation of musical references found in the literature of antiquity, has proved undoubtedly the most useful of the three general methods. As long ago as the eighteenth century the musical historians Charles Burney and Sir John Hawkins were able to write at length on the music of antiquity, deriving their entire evidence from references to music in ancient literature. Relying on such literary evidence, Burney wrote more than five hundred pages and Hawkins almost as many describing the music of the Hebrews, Greeks, and Romans.

One instrument of the ancient Hebrews still survives in modern use, the *shofar* or ramshorn. Although only two notes can be sounded on the shofar, the tonic and the fifth, the various blasts blown at such solemn times as Rosh Hashonah and Yom Kippur can powerfully affect the emotions. The tone-quality is sharp and penetrating, the rhythmic patterns of the blasts incisive, and even more powerful is the impact of the blasts when the listener remembers the association of the shofar with Biblical events.

One event among many when its use is recorded was the taking of Jericho. Joshua, the Hebrew leader, commanded his troops to march with the priests seven times round the walls of Jericho. The first six times they marched silently, according to the narrative, but at the seventh time the priests blew their rams' horns fortissimo, whereupon 'Joshua said to the people, Shout; for the Lord hath given you the city.'

None of the other Jewish instruments used in antiquity has survived in continuous use. One reason is that until the last hundred years no instruments but the shofar were permitted in synagogue services. Pictorial representations have very rarely been found, because the Hebrews themselves, in obedience to what they conceived to be a divine mandate, did not practise the visual arts. Occasionally we find a picture of a Hebrew instrument, such as that of the ten-stringed 'asor, somewhat resembling the modern zither, depicted on a Phoenician ivory box now in the British Museum. On the Triumphal Arch of Titus erected in Rome after the destruction of Jerusalem in A.D. 70 were carved in bas-relief several ceremonial objects used in the Temple, among them being the silver trumpets two feet in length, called hatzotzerah, which were played on festal occasions.

If one were reduced, however, to this type of evidence

alone, present-day knowledge of ancient Hebrew music would be meagre indeed. References to music in the Bible tell more, and from them several general conclusions can be drawn concerning the uses to which it was put in Biblical times. As far as Old Testament references are concerned: (1) music appears to have been used frequently as an emotional stimulant; (2) during the later periods of Israelitic history it would seem to have been professionalized; (3) instrumental music, especially after the exile, appears to have been as important as vocal music.

In hours of crisis the national hopes and fears seem naturally to have expressed themselves in music. At the time of the Red Sea crossing (*Exodus* 15), the deliverance was celebrated in a triumphal ode sung by Moses. Meanwhile Miriam, his sister, 'took a tambourine in her hand' and sang responsively with the Hebrew women the victory song. Deborah's song (*Judges* 5) and David's playing before the ark when he brought it to Jerusalem (*II Samuel* 6) afford further examples of the way in which music entered into Hebrew life. 'All the house of Israel played before the Lord on all manner of instruments made of fir wood, even on harps, and on psalteries, and on timbrels, and on cornets, and on cymbals.'

David's playing of the harp for Saul is a famous story. Whether the *kinnor* he played was a harp or a lyre, the point is the same: Saul's madness was assuaged by music. On another occasion (*I Samuel* 10: 5–6) Saul was 'turned into another man' when he heard a band of prophets playing on 'a psaltery, and a tabret, and a pipe, and a harp'. The prophet Elisha was yet another Old Testament character who was raised to a state of ecstasy by the sound of a minstrel's playing (*II Kings* 3: 15). References of this type may perhaps seem of small importance today, but in former centuries when the authority of the Bible was frequently invoked they convinced the learned that music could elevate man's spirit to the divine, and helped to confer upon it a much more lofty status than it would have had if it had been regarded solely as a means of inducing pleasure.

Such solemn events as that described in *II Chronicles* 5 have been frequently invoked as precedents by those who have advocated similarly large expenditures for music in Christian ceremonies. Nehemiah's insistence that the rebuilt walls be dedicated with 'cymbals, harps, and lyres', and his summoning of members of the guild of singers to the dedication ceremonies may now seem small details in the story as it appears in *Nehemiah* 12. But in former centuries, when the Church was the greatest patron of music, the Biblical precedents for expensive choirs, orchestras, and bands were of no small moment.

During the later epochs of Hebrew history music became a profession whose ranks were closed to all save those born into a particular clan in the tribe of Levi. David is credited with organizing the Temple singers, and is said to have 'set apart for the service certain sons of Asaph, Heman, and Jeduthun, who should prophesy with lyres, harps, and cymbals.' There were to have been 288 'skilful' musicians 'instructed in singing to the Lord.'[1] Moreover they were required to take turns in the exercise of their functions: 'they cast lots for their duties, the small as well as the great, the teacher as the pupil.' The beginnings of a Temple school of sacred music where master and student worked together as members of a co-ordinated guild can be discerned in this passage. The Temple musicians were profes-

---

[1] *I Chronicles* 25: 7.

sionals, if we may accept the evidence in *I and II Chronicles*. Instrumental music, moreover, seems to have played a dominant role in the ritual acts described in the Psalms. *Psalm* 150 speaks of praising God 'with the blast of the horn, . . . with the lyre and lute, . . . with the drum and dance, . . . with strings and pipe, . . . with clanging cymbals, . . . and with clashing cymbals.'

In the New Testament, Temple ceremonies as such are not described. Jesus is spoken of as having visited the Temple at the age of twelve, and as having revisited it on numerous occasions during later life. 'He taught in the Temple every day' during the Last Week, according to *Luke* 19: 47. The apostles in the *Acts* are also spoken of as having frequently attended Temple ceremonies. But specific references to music are rarer in the New Testament than in the Old. Such stray references as the story of Jesus's sending away the musicians before raising the daughter of Jairus, or the story of the elder brother's displeasure on hearing music and dancing in the house when the prodigal son returned, tell us little concerning its role in New Testament life. It is recorded that Jesus and His disciples sang a hymn before they went to the garden of Gethsemane. This is the only reference to His having sung, but it was of considerable importance in later Christian history, since the precedent was always invoked for the practice of singing the liturgy.

Instrumental music is scarcely mentioned in the New Testament. St. Paul's somewhat pejorative reference to 'sounding brass and tinkling cymbal' has been taken as an implied warning against all instrumental music. The fact that it was not specifically mentioned as a part of Christian worship either in the gospel narratives or in St. Paul's writings has been interpreted, at various times in Christian history, as an implied ban on all instrumental music in Church ceremonies. Undoubtedly during the first two centuries while Christianity was fighting for its very existence, instrumental music, or elaborate music of any type, was out of place. Only when it emerged from the catacombs was the Church ready to call upon professional musicians for an elaborate ritual of music involving instruments as well as singing.

St. Paul mentioned singing in *Ephesians* 5: 19 and *Colossians* 3: 16, but in each instance he called upon the infant Christian communities to give first place in their musical exercises to the singing of psalms. He also suggested that music should be used as an aid to teaching, calling upon his converts to 'teach and admonish each other in psalms, hymns, and spiritual songs.' He clearly favoured music as a pedagogic aid, but never as a merely sensuous delight. Following his example, most early Christian writers spoke disparagingly of music when its aim was merely the giving of pleasure.

In classic Greek thought, as in Pauline Christianity, music which merely pleased and excited was disparaged. According to the theories enunciated in Plato's *Republic* (Book III), Aristotle's *Politics* (Book VIII), Polybius's *Histories* (Book IV), and Plutarch's *Morals* ('Concerning Music'), the desirable functions which music can perform include these three: (1) the stimulation of heroic action; (2) the moulding of character; (3) the inducing of rapture.

Ideally Plato thought of music as a stimulant to deeds of heroism, and he therefore condemned such instruments as the oboe–like *aulos* because he feared their debilitating effect upon character. He recognized that certain types of music have the power of transporting a listener into desirable states of physical rapture, but he never adopted the hedonist's view that music divorced from moral ends has a right to existence. Aristotle taught that in rhythm and melody may be discerned imitations of the various traits in human character:

> Rhythm and melody supply imitations of . . . qualities of character. . . . Even in mere melodies there is an imitation of character, for the musical modes differ essentially from one another. . . . Some of them make men sad and grave, like the so-called Mixolydian [mode], others enfeeble the mind, . . . another, again, produces a moderate and settled character, which appears to be the peculiar effect of the Dorian; the Phrygian inspires enthusiasm.   (*Politics* 1340 *a–b*)

Both Plato and Aristotle alike banned the so-called Lydian mode, which roughly corresponded to what we now know as the major scale. They considered it to induce softness and to weaken the urge towards heroic deeds. Milton, in *L'Allegro*, followed Aristotle in ascribing to the Lydian mode a wanton influence.

> *Lap me in soft Lydian airs,*
> .   .   .   .   .
> *Of linkèd sweetness long drawn out,*
> *With wanton heed, and giddy cunning.*

The number of pieces of Greek music which we still possess is surprisingly meagre. Only some five or six have come down to us from antiquity. The most valuable of them are two Hymns to Apollo inscribed on the temple walls at Delphi; these are thought to have been written about 130 B.C. Among the other fragments are a Hymn to Nemesis and two Hymns to the Muse.

The Greek modes were descending rather than ascending patterns of scale-steps. The starting-note of the scale was the highest, and the intervals were counted downwards instead of upwards. As in our scales, there were seven letter-name notes within the Greek octave. The octave was in turn divided into tetrachords, that is to say groups of notes bounded by the perfect fourth. The Dorian mode meant approximately the descending series of notes we should encounter if we began on an E on the piano and played down the white notes to the next lower E. The Greek Phrygian meant the scale pattern which approximates to the descending series of notes from D to the next lower D. The Lydian mode meant the descending pattern we might encounter playing from C to the next lower C.[1]

The terms chromatic and enharmonic, though used in treatises on Greek musical theory, did not have the same significance that they have nowadays. In the chromatic modification of a Greek mode the seven notes in the octave were so disposed that two augmented seconds were introduced into the scale. Thus a descending scale of the chromatic type might read A—Gb—F—E—Db—C—B—A. The enharmonic modification employed by the Greeks cannot be even approximated in modern notation. As the Greeks knew the term enharmonic, it referred to scales containing smaller intervals than the smallest we now use.

[1] For further information on the Greek scales, see Curt Sachs, *The Rise of Music in the Ancient World*, pp. 225-237. The explanation of Greek Dorian, Phrygian, and Lydian in the above paragraph is the conventional one, but has been contested.

The Greeks themselves in their later Hellenistic and Roman periods gave up the enharmonic genus with its extremely minute intervals. Plutarch, writing at the end of the first century A.D., said that in former times only the enharmonic genus had been favoured in theoretical discussions.

> Of the three genera into which the musical scale is divided, ... one only was cultivated by the ancients. In their treatises we find no direction given on the use of the diatonic genus or the chromatic, but of the enharmonic alone.

Plutarch added, however,

> Our contemporaries [A.D. 100] have thoroughly neglected the finest genus, to which the ancients devoted all their eagerness. Most of them [our contemporaries] have lost the discernment of enharmonic intervals.

Other evidence could be added to show that in the decline of Greek civilization musical taste changed and that in the later period the enharmonic genus was abandoned.

Although the surviving fragments of Greek music have all been transcribed into modern notation, the correct pitches for the various Greek letter-named notes still remain undecided. The Greeks knew nothing of a five-line staff on which round notes with stems attached tell the performer not only what pitches to sing, but also how long to sustain each pitch. Instead they used letters from an obsolete alphabet. The same letter could appear in three different positions, erect, on its side, or upside down. Each position told something about the highness or lowness of the note in question. The letter upside down, for instance, meant to sharpen the note, that is, to raise its pitch.

The letter-names do not tell, however, what the exact pitch of the letter-name C was, or the exact pitch of the letter-name E or F. These letter-names, it is true, were used in Greek music, but C, as the Greeks used it, did not mean the C that we hear when we play middle C, or C the octave above, on the piano. C in ancient Greek notation may arbitrarily have sounded at any rate of vibration which suited the performer's convenience. Absolute pitch in our sense was yet unborn. A letter-name in Greek music, therefore, as in Gregorian music, in no sense revealed the exact pitch (rate of vibration) of any particular note, but rather told only where the note in question fitted into a preconceived pattern of scale-steps.

Most of the fragments of Greek music which remain have been transcribed into modern notation with time-signatures of $\frac{5}{4}$ or $\frac{5}{8}$. Music in quintuple metre is today almost as rare as a building in the shape of a pentagon. But if we understand the ancient fragments correctly, the Greeks had an especial fondness for rhythmic patterns involving fives.

Whether the Greeks ever sang their melodies in any other way than in unison throughout cannot now be known. Our evidence does not permit us to say that they ever sang or played their music *designedly* in such a way that, at one and the same instant, several different sounds with different letter-names could be distinguished. In our music today we demand chords — simultaneous combinations of musical notes. A single voice alone, or even several voices and instruments playing an unadorned tune throughout an entire piece of music, we do not find impressive. The ancients, however, seem not to have shared our fondness for chords. Just as we dislike hearing three or four people all trying to talk at the same time, and all saying different things, so the ancients seem to have disliked music in which there were several 'parts' going on at once. Certainly they had no harmony in our sense of the term, and any chords that may have occurred in their music did not result from the independent movements of the different voices. If occasionally intervals other than the octave were heard, they must have been the result of accident rather than of any clearly formulated plan.

In *Troilus and Cressida*, Pandarus asks a servant what music is being performed, and the servant replies, 'I do but partly know, sir; it is music in parts.' But in this passage Shakespeare was indulging in one of his frequent anachronisms.

If anyone were to ask us today what we know about ancient music, we might justifiably reply that what little we do know is but partly known. One thing, however, we are sure of: ancient music was *not* music in parts. That innovation was reserved for the Middle Ages. The most important single development in medieval music was, in fact, the development of polyphony, which is the art of combining several different independent melodies so that the singers can all be singing their different parts, but in such a way as to produce an agreeable effect upon the listener.

Supplementary Readings
The New Oxford History of Music, Vol. I, edited by Egon Wellesz, promises to be authoritative.

The Rise of Music in the Ancient World, by Curt Sachs, provides the best one-volume treatment of the topics in this chapter that is available at the present moment.

Grove's Dictionary of Music and Musicians, 5th edition, article on *Greek Music (Ancient)*.

CHAPTER II

MUSIC IN THE MEDIEVAL CHURCH

The idea that music should be entertaining, and could properly have only one end in view — the giving of pleasure — was as much frowned upon by the early Christian Fathers as it had been by the ancient Greek moralists. When St. Augustine was moved to tears while listening to Church music, he immediately checked himself and questioned whether he had committed sin. In Book 10, Chapter 33, of his *Confessions*, he expressed himself thus:

> Sometimes I am very fierce in the desire of having the melody of *all pleasant music*, to which David's Psalter is so often sung, banished both from my ears, and out of the whole church, too.

Augustine then commended the practice of the Church of Alexandria, where the ascetic Athanasius had succeeded in confining its music to a very few melodies so simple as to be scarcely more than inflected monotones. He concluded: 'So oft as it befalls me to be more moved with the beauty of the voice than with the words themselves, I confess myself to have grievously offended.'

From the very beginning of Christian history, there was singing in the Church. Even as early as the time of Pliny the Younger (A.D. 113) Christians were gathering before daybreak in order to sing hymns to Christ as God. The oldest surviving piece of Christian music is a hymn in praise of the Holy Trinity inscribed on papyrus in Egypt about A.D. 275. The melody, written in Greek letter notation, though covering only an octave compass has a notably fine sweep. According to Dr. Egon Wellesz, 'No other piece of Greek music has come down to us which has so rich a flow of melody.'

The age of other early Christian melodies which we possess is difficult to judge, but some of them, at least, must be extremely ancient. One way of judging their age is to examine the version of Scripture used as text. St. Jerome (340–420) is generally credited with the version known as the Vulgate. But a version in Latin, the Itala, existed before Jerome's time; it naturally differs somewhat from his. Therefore a melody in the repertory of Catholic Church song with words in the old Itala version, rather than in Jerome's newer Vulgate, was most probably composed before the latter became the accepted version in the Church.

By the end of the sixth century A.D., the repertory of Church song had evidently grown quite large. The diversities which existed throughout Western Europe in the singing of the melodies about the year 600 seem to have provoked the statesman-Pope, Gregory I (590–604), to institute several important reforms. Among these, he is credited with the organization of a Schola Cantorum, a school of singers in which youths could be trained in the singing of the Church repertory. At that early epoch the kind of musical notation which we use to designate pitch and duration had not come into existence, and the learning of the Church melodies was largely accomplished by the laborious process of memorization. Master taught pupil, and then pupil went out to a distant place in order to become himself a teacher of other pupils. The founding of a Schola Cantorum, whether by Gregory I or another, was a wise step, in that the traditions of Rome, itself an ancient centre of Christian life, could thereby be perpetuated and transmitted through alumni who carried with them the traditions of early Christian usage.

Some medieval writers thought that Gregory not only helped to unify customs relating to music, but was also a composer, who added his own melodies to the already existing repertory of Church song. Because of his far-reaching influence in the work of standardization, the whole body of Catholic Church music composed during the Middle Ages for single voice line has come to be known as *Gregorian Chant*.

These are the typical traits of Gregorian Chant: (1) the melodies are designed for a single voice line; (2) the rhythms of the music are the rhythms not of regular poetic patterns but of prose; (3) the music is designed not to titillate the senses but to move the hearer's heart and mind to worship; (4) the scales used do not conform to our modern scale patterns, but rather are cast in what were called *modes*.

Taking up these traits singly, one notices first the absence of chords or accompaniment. Nowadays when Gregorian Chant is sung, an organ is often brought in to accompany and support the voices. This use of the organ as accompaniment contravenes, however, the practice of the Middle Ages.

The rhythm of modern music is the rhythm of poetry, with the regular pattern of stresses in the line that poetry implies. Gregorian Chant follows no such pattern. In the thirteenth century it came to be known as *musica plana*, a term translated into English as plainsong or plainchant and implying music in the free rhythm of prose. The duration of each individual note in Gregorian melodies was in most cases, it is now asserted, equal. A medieval writer on music by the name of Jerome of Moravia (who flourished around 1270) said 'all notes are of equal value with a few exceptions'. His exceptions included such notes as the last notes at the ends of phrases (where the text would receive punctuation).

Rhythm to most of us nowadays has the connotation of alternating heavy and light beats. An interesting rhythm, many now think, implies accent. The sound of marching feet and the beat of the drum, for instance, mean rhythm to many of us. By these standards Gregorian music lacks rhythmic impulse. Its rhythm is that 'of the wind blowing through the trees or of a stream running over pebbles'. Its basic impulse, as analysed by musical scholars, is an impulse upward rather than a beat downward. Whereas a footfall marks a beat with us, in Gregorian Chant the rhythmic pulse is felt as a sweep upward. This difference in rhythmic concept can perhaps be best illustrated by a brief reference to the practice of conductors.

A conductor of an orchestra nowadays lets his hand fall on the principal, that is to say, the beginning beat of each measure. The Gregorian conductor, however, does not let his hand fall at the beginning of each rhythmic group: rather he lifts his hand. The rhythmic energy occurs thus at the moment of take-off, not at the moment of return to earth after the flight. This whole Gregorian concept of rhythm, whether as taught by scholars of the Solesmes school or by others, is so basically antithetical to most modern notions that very few untrained listeners can grasp it without giving it considerable attention.

The third general trait of Gregorian music is its 'functional character'. Everyone knows what is meant by incidental music — music designed to heighten the mood of a play, for instance, and to induce a succession of emotional responses suitable to the action on the stage. In a certain sense, Gregorian music is also incidental music. It is music incidental to the main business of the Church, which is worship. At its best it focuses the listener's attention on the liturgical action.

The fourth general observation concerning Gregorian music has to do with the modes in which the melodies are cast. Mode, as far as Gregorian music is concerned, means a ladder of eight successive notes (an 'octave'), so arranged that the rungs between the successive notes in the scale form either whole- or half-steps. The patterns of whole- and half-steps differ for each mode. The medieval theorists called their modes by names which the Greeks had already used. But the Church theorists meant different patterns by the same names. In the writings of medieval theorists we find an attempt made to divide the entire repertory of Gregorian melodies according to a preconceived scheme of eight modes; the odd-numbered modes (I, III, V, VII) were called 'authentic' in this scheme, and the even-numbered modes (II, IV, VI, VIII) 'plagal'.

The concept of modes, though perhaps somewhat abstruse, is nevertheless worth our grasping. A student may go to the piano and play an ascending series of white notes, beginning with D in the middle of the piano and ending on D the next octave above. 'The series of notes which you have just played', an instructor would say, 'constitutes the *Dorian Mode.*' The arrangement of *whole-steps* and *half-steps* in the Dorian mode follows this pattern:

Degrees of scale	1	2	3	4	5	6	7	8
Intervening steps	Whole	½	Whole	Whole	Whole	½	Whole	
Names of notes	D	E	F	G	A	B	C	D

A student may then start on E and play the white notes ascending to the next E. 'That series of notes', the teacher would say, 'comprises the *Phrygian Mode*.' And then perhaps the teacher would supply another diagram with a different arrangement of whole-steps and half-steps.

Degree of scale	1	2	3	4	5	6	7	8
Intervening steps	½	Whole	Whole	Whole	½	Whole	Whole	
Names of notes	E	F	G	A	B	C	D	E

Looking at the diagrams the reader will notice that in the Dorian mode the half-steps occur between the second and third degrees of the mode and between the sixth and seventh degrees; but that in the Phrygian mode the half-steps occur between the first and second degrees and between the fifth and sixth degrees. The *place where these half-steps occur* is of prime importance in determining the mode's character. Instead of beginning on the note D the student can begin on any other note and play a Dorian scale, provided only that he arranges the ascending-note pattern in such a way that the whole- and half-steps conform to the pattern given above for the Dorian mode. Similarly with the other modes: any given mode can start anywhere, provided only that the appropriate pattern of successive whole-steps and half-steps is preserved. (The reader should, of course, remember that the piano did not exist when Gregorian music was being composed; it is now used as an aid only because it is handy, not because it is an entirely accurate guide.)

We may add here the patterns used in constructing the two remaining authentic modes, the Lydian and Mixolydian. To find a Lydian mode, play from F up to the next higher F, using white notes. The Lydian pattern of whole- and half-steps follows:

Degrees of scale	1	2	3	4 5	6	7 8
Intervening steps	Whole	Whole	Whole	½	Whole	Whole ½
Names of notes	F	G	A	B C	D	E F

To find a Mixolydian scale start on G, and play the ascending series of white notes up to the next G. The Mixolydian pattern of whole- and half-steps will then occur:

Degrees of scale	1	2	3 4	5	6 7	8
Intervening steps	Whole	Whole	½	Whole	Whole ½	Whole
Names of notes	G	A	B C	D	E F	G

The term *authentic*, as we use it in relation to a Church mode, means simply that any melody thus classified is so constructed that all (or most of) the notes lie above the last note in the melody, the *final*. There are four authentic modes, the Dorian, the Phrygian, the Lydian, and the Mixolydian. There are another four modes, called *plagal*, which bear the names of *Hypo*dorian, *Hypo*phrygian, *Hypo*lydian, and *Hypo*mixolydian. These are thought to have developed somewhat later than the authentic modes.

Tradition has it that St. Ambrose, Bishop of Milan from 374 to 397, was the first to initiate hymn-singing in the West using melodies in the authentic modes. Melodies in the plagal modes are supposed to have appeared much later. In general, we may say that the notes of a plagal melody tend to lie around the note on which the melody ends, *above and below* the final note, whereas the notes in an authentic melody mostly lie *above* the final.

The point in a melody where the voice comes to a momentary breathing-place (which occurs where punctuation in the text demands a short pause) is called a *cadence*. In an authentic melody the final cadence will naturally call for a descending curve in the voice line, since the final note is a bottom note. In a plagal melody the final cadence may, on the other hand, occur simultaneously with an ascent in the voice line. The psychological effect upon the listener of a melody which finds its ultimate resolution in a low note is apt to be somewhat different from that of a melody which pushes its way upwards to its final note.

One other difference between authentic and plagal melodies is worth observing. Gregorian melodies tend to pivot round a note called the dominant[1] of the mode. The *dominant* may be compared to a perch on the bough of a tree to which the melody clings before returning to its nesting-place. Without waiting for a Gregorian melody to fly back to its final note, one can usually tell what mode it belongs to simply by watching the particular perch upon which it seems to sit and brood before descending. The perch to which a Dorian melody will cling will be differ-

---

[1] The dominant, or *confinalis,* is the fifth degree of authentic modes and a third lower for corresponding plagals, except that the note *B* if required by this rule is replaced by *C*.

ent from that on which Hypomixolydian melodies will rest.

The great majority of Gregorian melodies from the primitive period belong to the Dorian and Phrygian modes. A distinguishing trait of both these modes is the whole step between the seventh and eighth degrees of the scale. The modern ear finds a whole step between the seventh and eighth degrees of the scale unsatisfactory and somehow disillusioning. Since we prefer a half-step (semi-tone) between the seventh and eighth degrees, both the harmonic minor and the ascending melodic minor sharpen (i.e. raise) the seventh degree.

This desire for a half-step, deeply embedded in our musical subconscious, is a longing unfulfilled in Gregorian music. Because of this, Gregorian melodies in the Dorian and Phrygian modes seem elusive and ethereal to most of us. They seem to end with a wistful feeling, like that in the familiar quotation from Scripture: 'For here have we no continuing city, but we seek one to come.'

Gregorian music, though recognized as vitally important in an historical sense, has not been over-popular in our generation even in the Roman Catholic Church, with its long tradition of Gregorian chanting and with its official policy endorsing such music. Undoubtedly the number or places where one can hear Gregorian chant well rendered today are limited. A few gramophone records are, however, available; the best performances are perhaps to be found in recordings made by the monks of Solesmes in France.

Over a century ago a group of Benedictine monks at Solesmes Abbey began the difficult task of removing from Gregorian chant the encrustations which had settled upon it during the course of centuries. By this time these were so thick that not even the most conscientious student could make a proper interpretation. With infinite patience the monks gathered together the originals or photographic copies of all known medieval manuscripts containing Gregorian melodies. They used a single guiding principle in deciding what constituted the pristine contour of a plainsong melody, the greatest number of manuscripts with the same reading determining the authentic form. They have now achieved a striking success in their efforts to remove the tarnish from the melodies and to restore them to their former austere beauty.

In 1903 Pope Pius X approved the labours of the Solesmes monks and recommended their editions of chant for use throughout the Roman Catholic Church. In his encyclical letter *Motu Proprio* issued in that year, he stated that the ideal music for use in Church services was in his judgment either Gregorian chant or music modelled on Gregorian prototypes. A representative collection of Gregorian melodies will be found in the *Liber Usualis . . . in recentioris musicae notulas translatum*, issued in Belgium by Desclée & Cie at Tournai. The original melodies were written, however, in what is called *neumes*, the ancestors of modern musical notation, and the same selection of melodies is therefore given in another edition of the *Liber Usualis* in neumes for use in monastic houses and by scholars.

The history of notation is an important branch of musical history, for notation serves the same purpose for music as writing does for literature. Just as a people who have no system of writing are handicapped in preserving the ideas of the past and can develop only a limited culture, so a people who have no adequate system of musical notation cannot make much progress in nurturing music. Only a comparatively small number of melodies can be memorized and transmitted orally, and traditions that are merely oral are at best a precarious link with the past.

In the early stages of music in Western Europe, no better system of notation had been devised than the use of letters of the alphabet to indicate the pitch of successive notes in the melody. This cumbersome method gave place in time to a system in which a horizontal line indicating a fixed pitch-level was used. The first horizontal line used in medieval manuscripts for this purpose was coloured red and represented the note F. In time a second line, usually yellow but sometimes green, was added, representing the note C. A note above the F-line in this system might, however, represent either G, A, or B, and a note above the C-line might represent either D or E. In order to avoid ambiguity, the idea of using a four-line staff eventually took hold. With the lines representing alternate letter-name notes of the musical alphabet, and the spaces between representing the others, absolute clarity at last became possible. The invention of the four-line staff has been attributed to an Italian Benedictine monk, Guido d'Arezzo (995–1050), but upon insufficient evidence. In any case, his other musical accomplishments were so noteworthy that in the course of time he became a fabulous figure, credited with all the musical improvements that occurred throughout the entire Middle Ages. Like Jubal in the Book of Genesis, Guido became known as 'the father of all such' as are musically accomplished.

In looking through the index of the *Liber Usualis* one finds the melodies classified under such headings as 'hymns', 'antiphons', 'sequences'. There are only five sequences, but since one of these is perhaps the most famous single example of medieval monody, the *Dies Irae*, it may profitably be studied in some detail. No other example of Gregorian chant has been more highly regarded and widely employed. Such famous nineteenth-century composers as Liszt, Berlioz, and Saint-Saëns used the *Dies Irae* melody as thematic material. In our own century Rachmaninoff has quoted snatches of it in his *Isle of the Dead* and in his *Rhapsody on a Theme by Paganini*, and Vaughan Williams has used it in *Five Tudor Portraits*.

The words are a free paraphrase of certain verses in the first chapter of the prophecies of Zephaniah, foretelling an imminent Judgment Day:

> That day is a day of wrath, a day of trouble and distress, a day of wasteness and desolation, a day of darkness and gloominess, a day of clouds and thick darkness, a day of the trumpet and alarm . . .

Zephaniah's prophecy was paraphrased by Thomas of Celano, a Franciscan friar, about the year 1250, in a long Latin poem comprising nineteen stanzas. To this some anonymous composer fitted a melody which, according to the *Harvard Dictionary of Music*, is 'one of the most impressive products' of the Middle Ages. In few melodies of any century can there be felt such a mood of inexorable finality.

The *Dies Irae* melody contains a large number of repeated phrases; the first 29 notes, for instance, are immediately repeated. Then the next 34 notes are sung and repeated. The next 33 notes are sung, and at once repeated. The plan of the melody may be thus outlined: [A¹ – A²;

$B^1 - B^2$; $C^1 - C^2$]; [$A^3 - A^4$; $B^3 - B^4$; $C^3 - C^4$]; [$A^5 - A^6$; $B^5 - B^6$; $C^5 - D - E$]. In this diagram each capital letter stands for a unit of the melody which fits one stanza in the poem. It is thus obvious that the melodic units are repeated not once but as many as six times for the first unit (A), six times for the second unit (B), and five times for the third unit (C). Though the last two stanzas of the melody are not repeated, yet they bear such a close relationship to all that has gone before that in a certain sense they seem to be a peroration, or summing up of all that has been heard. Even a cursory glance at the structural scheme shows how formally balanced are its component parts. The composer was in his own way as perfect a formalist as Mozart.

The idea of having two or more people sing together, but with each singing different pitches, seems to us today a simple one; why, then, did it take such a long time for musicians to stumble upon it?

The first clear evidence of part-singing comes to us from the ninth century, a period in European history not generally thought of as a time of significant progress in science or in the arts. The beginnings are found in *Musica Enchiriadis*, a Latin treatise in which the author described a practice which he called *organum*. Though not a new word, since it occurs frequently in the Vulgate, with the meaning of a musical instrument, *organum* is used in this treatise to designate a new practice—singing in parallel fourths or fifths.

By the ninth century a large quantity of Gregorian music had, of course, been composed; and around the traditional chant hovered a halo akin to that surrounding Scripture itself. The best tribute anyone could pay to Scripture after the age of 'revelation' had ended was the writing of a commentary upon Scripture. Similarly with chant: the best thing that could be done in the ninth century was to write a commentary upon it. The commentary at first was an added voice which sang exactly the same melody as the original Gregorian tune, but a fourth or a fifth lower. (As may be perceived, the only way to add a melody that will exactly duplicate another but remain with the same scale system, or a closely allied one, is to put it at a distance of either an octave, a fourth, or a fifth. Singing in octaves can scarcely be considered part-music, but a melody at a fourth or fifth sounds as an added 'part'.)

After a period of singing chant with added parallel fourths or fifths, the next step in the history of polyphony involved the use of other intervals. Guido d'Arezzo in his treatise called *Micrologus* wrote that the added melody in this second stage of organum might go down where the Gregorian melody went up, and might go up where the original Gregorian went down. The voices were thus independent of each other in that they could move in opposite directions. But the intervals allowed between the two voices were still restricted to a small group of so-called 'consonances', or restful sounds.

'Dissonances', that is to say, tense sounds, were forbidden between the voices in the *Micrologus*. However, it is interesting to note that what Guido considered a consonance might not seem so to us to-day; and what we now consider consonance might, in the eleventh century, have been thought of as dissonance. Be that as it may, the intention during Guido's epoch was clear: composers merely added another melody that would sound always in perfect consonance (as they defined it) with the original Gregorian melody.

In the third stage of organum one finds for the first time marked rhythmic differences between the original Gregorian melody and the added 'composed' melody. In both the 'strict' organum of *Musica Enchiriadis*, and the 'free' organum of the *Micrologus*, the original melody and the added melody moved in lock-step in the same rhythmic patterns. A long note in the original was accordingly matched with a long note in the added, and a short note in the original with a short in the added. But with the advent of the third epoch in organum, in the twelfth century, we find the added melody now moving in a rhythm different from that of the original Gregorian melody. In the twelfth century, moreover, the Gregorian melody was no longer sung at the speed of speech, but instead its individual note-values were tremendously lengthened, while the added voice (now placed above) moved at a faster gait.

A remarkable school of composers arose at the Cathedral of Notre Dame in Paris during the twelfth century, among them Léonin and Pérotin; and it is with these two men that we begin at last in medieval music to encounter the names of individual composers. Léonin, perhaps a generation earlier than Pérotin, was evidently the outstanding master in the third stage of organum—that of 'melismatic' organum. Léonin wrote *organa* in which the Gregorian chant, submerged in the lowest part, and disguised by increasing extravagantly the length of each individual note, was reduced to the level of a bass drone. Over this Léonin placed a freely moving added melody that wandered about at a fast tempo.

The fourth stage (beginning of the thirteenth century) involved the 'measured' organum of Pérotin. Here the added melody or melodies (sometimes he added two parts above, sometimes three) danced about at a brisk tempo, usually in what we would call $\frac{6}{8}$ metre; pronounced accents were now felt, such as are found in all dance music. In Pérotin's compositions piquant rhythmic interludes, or *clausulae*, were introduced as episodes; during these the Gregorian chant no longer droned but was briskly fragmented.

In these *clausulae* Pérotin gave only the added voice part a text to sing. He seems to have expected his singers here to vocalize the original Gregorian melodies on some such open vowels as 'o-' or 'a-'. But during the century after Pérotin these 'Gregorian' voice parts were refurbished with added words, and these compositions were called motets. Thirteenth-century composers were of course not long content simply to add words to Pérotin's existing *clausulae*. Instead they composed their own motets.

The motet became an extremely 'wordy' composition during the thirteenth century, with texts sometimes in the vernacular and sometimes in Latin. Instead of only two voice parts one finds in the lively motets of the later thirteenth century three or four voices singing different melodies and different words. When two or three different sets of words were being sung simultaneously, no listener could have made sense of any of them. Perhaps, however, there was method in this madness. Often the motet texts were slightly on the improper side; the Gregorian chant fragments incorporated in a thirteenth-century motet were forced to undergo a strange metamorphosis. Reduced to small fragments in the *clausulae* of the Pérotin period, and then decked out with sometimes indecorous words in the thirteenth century, the chant melodies were forced into strangely flamboyant costumes during the epoch of Aquinas.

The year 1300 is often referred to as a watershed in the history of medieval polyphonic music, and the music of the fourteenth century is called *the new art*, or *Ars Nova*. Until the beginning of the fourteenth century, writers of polyphony had in general restricted themselves to commentary on previously existing melodies in the Gregorian repertory. But after 1300 composers began to write without using any *cantus firmus* ('fixed melody') derived from the older deposit.

Several developments occurred in *Ars Nova* which must be summarized here: (1) music became tremendously complicated rhythmically; (2) secular music became important; (3) intervals such as thirds, which had previously been considered dissonances, were now recognized as consonances; (4) dissonances, even when recognized as such, were used with considerable freedom; (5) the use of accidentals (flats and sharps) sharply increased.

In *Ars Nova* one finds great variety in rhythm; no longer does music in triple metre predominate. Pérotin's music had invariably been composed in triple metre, legend says because of an exaggerated deference for the number 3 — the number of the Trinity. But whatever the real reason for this may have been, the music of the fourteenth century burst the trammels of the preceding age, and duple metre came into common use. For the first time also one finds in *Ars Nova* frequent use of the device nowadays called syncopation. In the music of Guillaume de Machaut, a representative fourteenth-century composer (1300?–1377), the most varied rhythms are encountered in the individual parts. Machaut indeed achieved a degree of complexity in his rhythmic schemes that now taxes the most skilled vocal soloist.

A favourite device in Machaut is the principle of rhythmic repetition. This device, involving the repetition of the same rhythmic pattern in an individual voice part[1] several times during the course of a composition, but with a different melody each time, is called 'isorhythm'. Usually it is only after several hearings that the repeated rhythm can be discerned: an inner or lower voice repeating a complex rhythmic pattern while the upper voices pursue different patterns simply cannot be followed, even by the most acute listener, on first hearing. The effort of following the exact pattern of a single dancer, not a star, in a ballet company, who repeats his own particular routine while everyone else goes each his or her individual way, does not require any more concentrated attention than that of following with the ear the repeated rhythmic pattern of a lower voice in a Machaut isorhythmic motet.

As for the second development in the fourteenth century, the increasing importance of secular music: Machaut did, it is true, write a polyphonic Mass, and was probably the first composer who attempted the feat. But his Mass, said to have been written for the coronation of the Burgundian Charles V in 1364, is his only composition of its type; on the other hand, he wrote numerous motets (23 are still extant), and an impressive number of polyphonic ballades, rondeaux, and virelais. Though he was a priest, he spent most of his creative energy, judging from the remains of his output, on the composition of secular music rather than

---

[1] The voice most frequently organized along isorhythmic principles was the *tenor*.

sacred.[1] Most of his contemporaries in the time of the Avignon Popes occupied themselves similarly.

Concepts of consonance and of dissonance changed significantly during this period. Before 1300 fourths were considered consonances, but after that date they began to lose favour and were replaced by thirds. As a matter of interest, this shift is attributed to the influence of English music, in which a predilection for thirds had been shown as early as the twelfth century. During the thirteenth century an English composer had produced the famous round[2] *Sumer is icumen in*, in which thirds and sixths were used as favourite consonances. Continental composers followed the English precedent, importing into France and the Netherlands such characteristically English procedures as *gymel*, the practice of singing in parallel thirds. Finally, on the Continent during Palestrina's time (1525?–1594) fourths, which had been the first consonance recognized as such in organum, had fallen into such disfavour as to be relegated to the category of dissonances.

As for the last point, five accidentals were in common use after about 1325, C$\sharp$, E$\flat$, F$\sharp$, G$\sharp$, and B$\flat$. Occasionally an accidental is missing from a passage where the musical sense demands one. Medieval Church singers were professionals, however, and knew where custom required the use of an accidental. Scholars today must 'guess' where they should be added, and quite naturally their 'guesses' sometimes disagree.

In this section a whole millennium of musical history has been traversed in a necessarily cursory fashion. But medi-

---

[1] For Machaut's secular achievement see p. 65.
[2] Actually a *rota;* see p. 61.

eval music was as important a cultural achievement as was medieval architecture, and the reader may therefore wish to strengthen his background by studying such easily accessible examples as those contained in either Part I of the *Historical Anthology* (Harvard University Press) or in Arnold Schering's *Geschichte der Musik in Beispielen*. The student who wishes to see modern transcriptions of the music may also profitably examine a collection in the Eastman School of Music Series (University of Rochester) entitled *Examples of Music before 1400*, selected and edited by Harold Gleason. An extremely valuable account of medieval music for the serious student is to be found in Gustave Reese's *Music in the Middle Ages*. The *New Oxford History of Music,* Vols. 2 and 3, edited by Dom Anselm Hughes, provides the most recent and authoritative account. See also *Grove's Dictionary of Music and Musicians,* 5th edition: articles on *Ars Nova, Clausula, Modes, Motet, Notre-Dame School, Plainsong*.

CHAPTER III

SIXTEENTH-CENTURY SACRED
POLYPHONY

The Renaissance is regarded as an epoch of supreme achievement in sacred polyphony, and it is generally considered by historians of music that Josquin, Palestrina, Lassus, Victoria, and Byrd, with several others, achieved musical results which stand as counterparts to Michelangelo's frescoes and Raphael's paintings.

Bestriding the fifteenth and sixteenth centuries stands the musical colossus, Josquin des Prez (1450?-1521). Originally from the Flemish Netherlands, he early gained international renown. He found employment in the richest courts of Europe, at Milan in the 1470's, at Rome in the papal court from 1486 until 1494, at Paris and elsewhere as Louis XII's chapelmaster until 1515. After his death he was revered by such diverse men as Luther in Germany and Salinas in Spain as the greatest composer who had yet arisen. In 1567, nearly a half-century after his death, his star was still so bright that an Italian (Cosimo Bartoli in *Ragionamenti accademici*) thus summarized his importance:

Ockeghem [1420?-1495?] was, as it were, the first to rediscover music after it had almost completely died out, just as Donatello rediscovered sculpture. Josquin, Ockeghem's pupil, rightly deserves to be called a prodigy of nature, as far as music is concerned. Just as our Michelangelo Buonarotti stands first in architecture, painting, and sculpture, so Josquin stands first in music. Thus far

34

no one has even approached either of the two—Josquin in music or Michelangelo in the visual arts. They stand alone, without rivals, delighting all those who have any appreciation of the arts: and unique it appears they will remain into the distant future.

Not only was Josquin prominent; he was also genuinely popular with the public which bought early printed music. He was the first composer whose Masses were printed in a separate publication (by Ottaviano de' Petrucci in 1502). During his lifetime three such books, containing 17 of his Masses, were printed. His motets[1] were even more popular. Over 100 were printed in collections during his lifetime and the generation immediately following.

He was equally versatile as a sacred and secular composer. In his motets, which are the most esteemed category of his sacred compositions, he followed two main courses. Either he drew some ancient fragment of Church melody through the motet, like a strand of white yarn through a piece of multi-coloured knitwork, or he took the text and divided it where punctuation occurred, constructing the music for each phrase of text as if it were a separate square in a patchwork quilt. He was fond of sequences, that is, repetitions of melody higher or lower than the original statement, and in the same voice. At times he resorted to strong rhythmic accents, or conflicting accents in different voices, in order to enforce the emotional meaning. Whatever techniques he chose to employ, his music showed infinite variety of texture, of light and shade.

Beside him, such contemporaries as the Dutch Jacob

[1] The word *motet*, like the word *madrigal*, changed its meaning between the thirteenth and sixteenth centuries.

Obrecht (1450?–1505), the Flemish Heinrich Isaac (1450?–1517), and the Flemish Pierre de la Rue (?–1518), to name only three, seem minor figures. Just as Beethoven bestrode the eighteenth and nineteenth centuries, overshadowing all others, so Josquin three centuries earlier took precedence over the most talented of his contemporaries.

The standards of vocal art in sixteenth-century churches were perhaps higher than they have ever been since that time. Membership of Duke Albert's choir in Munich, where Lassus spent the greater part of his productive life; the Chapel Royal choir, for which Byrd wrote his Services; the Julian choir, for which Palestrina composed; or the choir of the Convent of Royal Barefoot Nuns, for which Victoria composed. was a coveted distinction, and was well paid. The singers, moreover, had a status similar to that of present-day orchestral performers. Just as the latter are nowadays paid to devote their entire energies to their orchestral work, so choral singers in the sixteenth century were paid to do nothing but sing. The same prestige that now attaches to membership of the best orchestras belonged then to membership of the choirs maintained by the principal foundations.

The organization of sixteenth-century choirs was framed within an elaborate system of rules concerning pay, absences, pensions, sick leave, conduct, bearing, and any number of more minute matters. Choirs to-day are most often composed of amateurs who either give their services or receive a mere token payment; but in earlier times they were as a rule highly professional bodies. One can hardly hope now for the polish and finish that were then regularly attained in choral performances. As an example of the extremely elaborate framework of rules governing members of such choirs, the *Constitutions of the Papal Chapel*, framed in 1545 at the instance of the zealous Paul III, may be examined: the fifty-nine chapters in this set of rules covered every conceivable aspect of a singer's life. The rule-book of any musicians' union today could not be more specific. The *Constitutions* were, moreover, directed towards one end — the maintenance of a rigid discipline. The vocal refinements of the Papal Chapel made possible by this discipline were imitated throughout the world; as far away as Mexico City, for instance, the standards of choral art were during the sixteenth century at a higher level than they have reached in any later century.

The composers after 1530 who must be reckoned with in any survey of the period were not by any means all centralized in one small area. In other centuries the principal composers have all congregated in one spot. During the latter part of the eighteenth century, for instance, the principal composers were to be found in Vienna. During the 1830's they gravitated to Paris, then later in the nineteenth century Vienna again became the dominant music capital. During the early part of our own century Paris once more was the magnet for the most significant talents. But in the sixteenth century, for one reason or another, music in its most refined aspects was not centralized as it is today, for instance, in New York or London. Rome was then a centre, but so was Seville with Francisco Guerrero, Toledo with Cristóbal de Morales, Madrid with Victoria, Mexico City with Hernando Franco, to name only a few composers in the Spanish orbit as examples. British music was at its zenith during this century, and although London eventually attracted the greatest names, nevertheless one discovers important composers working elsewhere — John Taverner, Robert Johnson, Robert Carver and Thomas Weelkes, for instance. In no other period, perhaps, can one find so many truly outstanding composers so widely distributed.

The gathering of details concerning the lives of even the greatest sixteenth-century composers is often a difficult task. Most musical biographies of that era lack such spice as that provided by Chopin's romance with George Sand, Liszt's with the Comtesse d'Agoult, or Wagner's with Cosima. There was, it is true, the case of the composer Carlo Gesualdo, who murdered his wife and her lover in bed, but the lives of others of that period tend to make dull reading, particularly when only a few meagre factual details are available. Even the career of so illustrious a musician as Giovanni Pierluigi da Palestrina can hardly be said to provide material for an enthralling narrative.

When the name of a composer or writer becomes famous in the process of time, and no picturesque facts are really known about him, an accretion of legend starts to form. With other outstanding figures of Palestrina's own century, legendary lives have been built up: take, for instance, the case of Shakespeare, who is credited with deer-stealing simply because the little we know of his youth lacks the colour we would like it to have. With Palestrina the legendary tale of his 'saving Church music' by writing a special Mass for performance at the Council of Trent is endlessly repeated, simply because the documented facts of his life are not very interesting. As recently as 1917 an opera by Hans Pfitzner called *Palestrina*, repeating the same exploded legend, was performed in Munich. Palestrina certainly did write a Mass called *Missa Papae Marcelli* in which the words can be clearly understood. And it is also a fact that the Council of Trent on September 14, 1562, did promulgate a decree expelling music with profane words from the Church; but to say that at any time the Council considered the expulsion of all polyphonic music (as in the opera) is historically inaccurate. The most palpable error in the opera, however, is the assumption that a prince of the Church would have called upon Palestrina, and humbly with hat in hand have begged him, 'Won't you please, kind sir, write us a Mass with intelligible words, so that we can convince the other princes of the Church attending the Council that polyphonic music is suitable for continued use in the services of the Church?'

Nobody who knew anything of the actual status of musicians in the sixteenth century could have conjured up so distorted a picture. Palestrina was, in fact, the one who did the supplicating; a plate in his first book of Masses, for instance, shows him humbly on his knees before Pope Julius III, presenting the volume, and the first Mass in it, *Ecce sacerdos magnus*, obsequiously extols his patron. Composers in Palestrina's day considered themselves lucky if they could find patrons willing to be bowed to; and the idea that a composer during that century could have achieved such social importance as that of Igor Stravinsky or even George Gershwin and Jerome Kern in our own day, is egregiously anachronistic.

Palestrina was luckier than most composers of his time, largely because he succeeded in obtaining as his patrons not mere princelings, but Popes, cardinals, and powerful dukes. His obsequiousness, moreover, knew no bounds. When he

published his first volume of Masses he directed the printer
to place a woodcut of Julius III's coat-of-arms wherever
that Pope's identifying theme, *Ecce sacerdos magnus*, appeared.

Julius III had been a bishop in the very town, some
twenty miles from Rome, in which Palestrina[1] had spent
his youth; he had been Julius's cathedral organist. Soon
after he became Pope Julius brought Palestrina to Rome.
First he made him master of the Julian choir, and then in
1555 installed him, much to the chagrin of the other
singers, as a member of the Pontifical choir. Six months
after this appointment he was dismissed, for Julius III had
died, and 'now there arose up a new king which knew not
Joseph'.

Other patrons, however, were found, such as the powerful Cardinal Carpi (who was induced to act as godfather to
Palestrina's son, Rodolfo), and the fabulously wealthy
Cardinal Ippolito d'Este. Palestrina was also unusually
successful in business; his second wife's money helped to
establish him in the lucrative fur trade, and the proceeds
enabled him to publish his many later works. Between
1581 and 1594 he issued fifteen volumes of his own compositions, all at his own expense. His servile attitude towards his patrons, however, even after he had become
prosperous in his later fifties, is somewhat surprising, whatever allowance one makes for sixteenth-century social
structure. As late as 1584 we find the following passage in
a letter to Duke Guglielmo Gonzaga:

I do not like to think that my work should reach other

[1] Palestrina is the name of the town in which the composer was born and
in which he served as a youthful organist. Many artists were known by the
name of their natal place during the sixteenth century.

hands before I had the benefit of that most prudent judgment of yours, such as none other possesses in this particular art of music; and had I been in your neighbourhood I should have liked to submit it to you for any suggestions as to improvement, before sending it to be printed.

What characteristics of sacred polyphony at mid-century strike us most forcibly today? In the first place, much of the music of the period sounds remote and ethereal. According to the canons of harmony in Palestrina's time, only what nowadays are called root-position triads and first-inversion chords were allowed to appear at the beginnings of measures. We must explain this in somewhat technical terms: no bar-lines were used in Palestrina's music, but any analysis will show that on the first and third 'beats' of measures in $\frac{4}{2}$ or on the first 'beats' in $\frac{3}{2}$, triads and first inversions only were used, except when suspensions were included. (A suspension is simply a delayed consonance.) The proportion of consonance was therefore much higher in sixteenth-century polyphony than it has been at any subsequent time.

A modern psychologist will tell us, on the basis of experimental evidence, that a consonance sounded at a certain volume always appears farther away than a dissonance at the same distance and of the same volume. Thus sixteenth-century sacred music with its addiction to consonances tends to sound remote. It is as if the music were conversing with the God whom the prophet Isaiah saw in a vision, when he 'saw also the Lord sitting upon a throne, high and lifted up, and his train filled the temple.' This feeling of Deity 'high and lifted up' is strongly suggested in sixteenth-century polyphony by the eternal round of pure consonances. Our feeling of estrangement is not simply the result of unfamiliarity with the Latin text or with the Gregorian melodies constantly reappearing in sixteenth-century music: more specifically it results from this constant basic pattern of consonances.

A second characteristic of sixteenth-century polyphony, a quality related to the sense of remoteness, is the absence of climax. Climax in composition can only be achieved if there is some effect of tension followed by resolution. In modern sacred favourites, such as the *Lord's Prayer* by Malotte, not only do we discover a large number of complex sounds such as seventh chords, but also a searching for climax. At the end when the singer rises to 'the kingdom, the power, and the glory', the very roof resounds with the notes of climax. But such climaxes were never sought by sixteenth-century composers. In Palestrina and Victoria they certainly do not occur, perhaps because 'heavenly' music was preferred to music with the theme of 'Marching to Zion'.

A third characteristic of sixteenth-century sacred music is the absence of strong rhythmic accents. There is no drum-beat in the ecclesiastical polyphony of those days. 'Onward, Christian soldiers, marching as to war,' is one of the most popular of modern hymns. Palestrina and Victoria published hymns for the whole Church year, but their hymns have no such martial spirit, and consequently cannot musically satisfy those who hope to march 'Onward'.

Other characteristics of ecclesiastical polyphony that deserve notice include (1) the treatment of the text; (2) the adaptation of existing melodies; and (3) a lack of emphasis upon originality. After having discussed these three further general points, we shall briefly list those musical features which are important in the technical analysis of the style.

Little attempt was made at word-painting. Words like 'anguish' or 'hate' were not necessarily illustrated in the music with an 'anguished' chord or 'hateful' dissonance. The downward swoop of a minor seventh at the opening of Tchaikovsky's song, 'None but the Lonely Heart', would not have been used to illustrate the anguish of loneliness. Palestrina's motet, *Surge, illuminare* (Third Book of Motets, 1575), does, it is true, start with a powerful surge, and the illumination bursts forth in the piling up of massed chords (this is a motet in eight voice parts). The concept 'And the glory of God is risen upon you,' found elsewhere in this book of motets, is as aptly illustrated as in Handel's much later *Messiah*. But word-painting in an excessive, overdrawn manner was not frequent in this earlier music.

Because the exact illustration of a sentiment in the text was not always considered important by the composer, one finds that a composition originally intended for one particular text was often divorced from it and wedded to another with quite a different meaning. If music originally written for other texts was thus remarried to portions of text in the Ordinary of the Mass, the result was known as a 'Parody Mass'. If only a 'tune' or *single* melodic line was borrowed, and used throughout, the result was a '*cantus firmus* Mass'. Occasionally popular tunes such as the famous French fifteenth-century folk-song, *L'homme armé*, were woven into the contrapuntal fabric of *cantus firmus* Masses, though usually in such altered form as to be completely unrecognizable. Because of abuses, however, any introduction of a secular tune into a Church composition was technically forbidden after 1563.

No great emphasis was placed upon originality for its own sake. Since composers did not cultivate an intensely personal idiom, authorship is sometimes in doubt. An example of this difficulty of identification is encountered in the 27 Responses for Holy Week, at one time attributed to Palestrina but now known definitely to have been composed by a lesser composer of the period, Marc' Antonio Ingegneri. It was only at the turn of the last century that a book printed in 1588 and bearing Ingegneri's name as composer came to light, proving conclusively his authorship of these Responses.

Today, people expect to recognize a contemporary composer by his individual style. In the sixteenth century, however, craftsmanship and sureness of technique were more important than the achievement of a markedly personal style.

A list of the more notable traits of sixteenth-century musical technique may serve as a short postscript to this general discussion. The only dissonances appearing at the beginnings of measures (or in the middle of $\frac{4}{2}$ measures) were always prepared by what we call suspensions. On the second and fourth pulsations in the measure ($\frac{4}{2}$ time) passing dissonances were allowed. Dissonances approached by a skip in the melodic line were not permissible. The top voice was not *the* melody, as it usually is today. Each voice was important, but, as far as the musical grammar was concerned, the lowest voice was the most important. All intervals and chords were counted from the lowest note upward, and the progressions of 'chords' were strictly controlled by what happened in the lowest voice. The chord progressions which were favoured were often related in their roots by an interval of a third, up or down. Another favourite chord progression was from one triad to another triad by step-wise movement in the roots. Modern harmony texts advise the student to avoid chord progressions where the roots are a third apart, especially over the barline. And such progressions as V–IV, IV–III, III–II, which were favoured in the sixteenth century, are not now approved. We favour I–II, or IV–V, but not the reverse.

Chord progressions were, of course, important to the sixteenth-century composer, just as they are now.[1] Palestrina, for instance, used to try his compositions over on a lute so that he could get the feel of the chord progressions. It is simply that our ideas of what constitutes good chord progression have changed. Sixteenth-century progressions must be studied to be appreciated; but they can be supremely satisfying after one has become accustomed to the sixteenth-century style. An oft-quoted example of a 'beautiful' chord progression is the beginning of Palestrina's *Stabat Mater* for eight voices. The first seven chords read as follows: A major, G major, F major, C major, F major, G minor, A major. During his early days as a conductor in Dresden Wagner came across this *Stabat Mater*, and praised it enthusiastically. He admired it so greatly that he made his own edition of it, which has helped enormously to popularize it with choral societies. Not only the interweaving of voices but also the harmonies pleased him. Schumann was another nineteenth-century composer who appreciated Palestrina's harmonic style; on one occasion he wrote:

At times it really sounds like the music of the spheres,

[1] Some theoreticians eschew the use of the words 'chord' or 'harmony' in discussing Palestrina's style. 'Chord' is used here to mean any simultaneous association of musical sounds that can be grammatically explained.

and then what art! I truly believe he is the greatest
musical genius ever produced in Italy.

During the sixteenth century, as we have already said,
musical genius was not a hothouse plant grown exclusively
in any one country. The Netherlands, France, England,
Germany, Spain — and even far-away Mexico — all produced outstanding composers during this most musical of
centuries. Tomás Luis de Victoria (1548–1611), the finest
composer Spain produced during the century, came from
Ávila, the birthplace of St. Teresa, and may have known
her personally. (In one of her books she mentioned
Agustín de Victoria, his brother.) In 1565 he went to
Rome, enrolling as a student in the Collegium Germanicum. Four years later he was appointed organist at the
Church of St. Mary of Montserrat, a Spanish church in
Rome, and in 1571 he succeeded Palestrina as chapelmaster
in the Collegium Romanum. Two years later he returned
to the Collegium Germanicum as singing master. On
28 August 1575 he was ordained priest. In 1578 he became
a chaplain at the Church of St. Jerome in Rome, and lived
during the next five years under the same roof with St.
Philip Neri, founder of the Oratorians. In 1579 Pope
Gregory XIII bestowed upon him a Spanish benefice that
did not require residence. In 1585 he ended his chaplaincy
at St. Jerome's Church, and was next appointed chaplain
to the widowed Empress Maria, Philip II's sister.

Victoria's first book of motets, published in 1572, was
dedicated to the Bishop of Augsburg. In 1576 he published
a large volume of miscellaneous compositions, including
five Masses and five Magnificats, dedicated to the Duke of
Bavaria. It is thus a striking fact that Victoria's earliest

patrons were Germans, not Spaniards or Italians. In his later life one volume after another appeared, culminating in the last of his printed works, a volume commemorating the Empress Maria, who died in 1603; this volume, entitled *Officium defunctorum sex vocibus in obitu et obsequiis Sacrae Imperatricis*, was published in a sumptuous edition at Madrid in 1605. For the last six years of his life Victoria seems to have been principally engaged in chaplaincy duties in the Madrid convent where he had taken up residence after returning from Italy. He died in 1611.

Both at Rome and in Madrid Victoria had excellent choirs at his disposal. His compositions published after his return to Spain were often written for double and triple choirs of eight and twelve voices. In Madrid, if we may judge from the resources which Victoria's later work presupposes, there existed choirs not inferior to those which Andrea and Giovanni Gabrieli, the most spectacular contrapuntists of the period, had at their disposal at St. Mark's in Venice. Antiphonal passages occur as readily in those of Victoria's compositions published after his return to Spain as they do with the younger Gabrieli.

Victoria, evidently for practical reasons, included in his 1600 volume published at Madrid an accompaniment for organ. In this book, however, the organ accompaniment is not an essential part of the musical fabric; it seems rather to have been inserted as a possible substitute for one of the antiphonal choirs, for smaller chapels where only one choir of polyphonic singers might be available. Chord progressions used for their appeal to the senses occur more frequently in Victoria's polyphony than in the music of Palestrina. It is strange that Victoria, whose world was more abstract than Palestrina's, should have brought a more passionate expressiveness to his music. To a modern listener Victoria, because of his harmonic sense, can be one of the most rewarding discoveries in sixteenth-century music.

In contrast to Palestrina, who wrote about 700 compositions, and Orlandus Lassus, who wrote about 1200, Victoria produced only 180. Unlike them, moreover, he confined his attention entirely to sacred music. And finally he did not often, as they did, weave into the fabric of his music popular secular ditties, such as *L'homme armé*, a temptation that in his greener years not even Palestrina was able to resist.

Orlandus Lassus (1532?–1594) was born at Mons in Flanders. He was thus heir to the achievements of a large school of important Flemish composers such as Ockeghem (fifteenth century), and Obrecht, Josquin des Prez and Pierre de la Rue (fifteenth and sixteenth centuries).

Like several of his musical predecessors from Flanders, Lassus emigrated to Italy at an early age. For three years he was in Naples, and later for a short period in Rome. A contemporary biographer writing of Lassus's stay in Rome says that he was appointed a choir director at the important church of St. John Lateran in 1553. In 1556 he received a call to the court chapel at Munich. He served there thirty-eight years, first under Albert V of Bavaria and later under his successor, William V. Soon after his arrival in Munich he was appointed head musical director, and his creative ambitions were thus given full scope. He was allowed periodic leave with pay to visit other important musical centres, where he enlarged his own outlook and recruited singers for the Bavarian chapel choir.

Under Lassus at one time there were 44 professional adult singers in the choir. Up to 1591, three years before Lassus's death, its membership never fell below 38, to which boy sopranos and altos would have been added. Not only had Lassus the backing of an excellent choir, but he was able to publish his compositions under the patronage of the Bavarian rulers, Albert and then William. In the dedication of *Patrocinium musices*, published in Munich in 1573, he wrote the following tribute to his patrons:

> The royal house of Bavaria has eminently served the cause of true piety in fostering music and in patronizing the publication of music. . . . The entire Christian world is indebted to the zeal and disinterestedness of the Duke of Bavaria.

In the same dedication Lassus stated his motives in composing and in publishing:

> It must be asserted at the very outset that all these compositions have been written with the one purpose of glorifying God. In His boundless goodness He desires that the blessing of corporate harmony may be ours, so that in our praise of Him we may enjoy the blessing of union amidst diversity: which the delicious harmony of many different voices blending together most aptly affords. . . . This music with which we praise Him ought less to arouse mere passing sensations of delight in us, than to arouse our vivid apprehension of the sacredness of the ceremonies to which the music belongs.

Lassus's reputation soon spread throughout Europe; in France he became a favourite among all classes. To suit French taste he wrote *chansons* with texts in gay and frivolous moods. So popular did these become, even among the most severe moralists, that in 1575 the Huguenots in La Rochelle decided to sing them, substituting sacred for secular words. They published their collection with a delightful title, *Mellange d'Orlande de Lassus contenant plusieurs chansons à quattre parties, desquelles la lettre profane a été changée en lettre spirituelle.*

Lassus wrote German *Lieder* as well as French *chansons*, and in addition composed a large number of madrigals with Italian texts. The madrigal was the predominant type of secular vocal music cultivated in Italy during the sixteenth century, and even Palestrina wrote ninety of them, though he later eschewed the form, criticizing it in the preface to the *Song of Songs*, 1584:

> There exists a vast mass of love-songs of the poets . . .
> songs of men ruled by passion; . . . they offend by their shallow taste.

On another occasion he spoke of 'those who devote their gifts to light and vain ideas'.[1] Certainly Lassus's work in his Italian madrigals tended at times towards the carefree and frolicsome, while even more shallow (and delightful) were certain of his minor compositions such as his *villanelle* and *moresche*.

But Lassus was never during his prolific career content merely to sit on the banks and sing

> *Come live with me and be my love*
> *And we will all the pleasures prove . . .*

His chromatic Italian madrigals, influenced in their style by

---

[1] After condemning the 'light vanities' of secular composition Palestrina nevertheless proceeded to publish a second volume of madrigals in 1586.

the bold experiments of Cipriano de Rore, an older Flemish contemporary resident in Italy during Lassus's sojourn there, were only one phase in his versatile career. In his later Munich manner Lassus refused, as had Palestrina before him, to sit

> *By shallow rivers, to whose falls*
> *Melodious birds sing madrigals.*

Lassus's command of Latin, French, Italian, and German is attested by the range of texts that he chose for his music and also by his use of these four languages in his personal correspondence. His letters written between 1572 and 1594, of which 52 have been preserved, contain a remarkable mosaic of phrases from all of them. In these letters, including a number written to Duke William, he reveals his intimate day-by-day experiences. He enjoyed a happy family life and was able to obtain advantageous musical appointments for his sons, three of whom survived him; as early as 1584 one of them was employed in the court chapel at an annual salary of 50 florins. Lassus's own salary after 1575 was 550 florins, with certain added perquisites that enabled him to live in handsome style. His letters mention his pleasures, his love of good eating, his fondness for mild outdoor sports, and particularly for fishing.

Some biographers have supposed that his growing austerity in later life, particularly his religious fervour, indicates a decline in his own zest for living, and have thought that his preoccupation with such texts as the *Lamentations of Jeremiah* (composed probably about 1585) proved his growing melancholia. But the fervour of William V, who succeeded Albert V in 1579, may have had much to do with Lassus's choice of sombre subjects during his last years. Towards the close of his life, in imitation of his patron, he cultivated the friendship of members of the Society of Jesus, and a portrait in the Jesuit Seminary at Munich shows that he won their esteem.

Perhaps the most famous of Lassus's more serious compositions is his series of *Penitential Psalms* (in the King James version those numbered 6, 32, 38, 51, 102, 130, and 143). Formerly it was thought that these superb settings were commissioned by Charles IX of France, as an expression of his repentance of the evil he had done at the Massacre of St. Bartholomew in 1572. They were published in 1584, but it is now known that they were composed twenty-four years earlier.

Lassus was known and admired not only in France and in Italy, but also during the 1590's in England, where Thomas Morley, the renowned Elizabethan madrigalist, caused a collection of Lassus's 24 two-part motets to be reprinted, under the title *Novae aliquot ad duas voces* (first printed in Munich in 1577). These motets are today widely used in elementary classes in counterpoint, as taught in *conservatoires* and in the music departments of colleges and universities. The part-writing in these comparatively simple motets for two voices is remarkably supple, and there are excellent pedagogic reasons for using them as examples for students to imitate. However, out of Lassus's 1200 compositions, only these 24 are for two parts, while all the rest are for three or more; thus his two-part motets represent no more than a small fraction of his total output. No composer can be rightly judged on the basis of only a few small works, no matter how exquisitely finished such miniatures may be. The works that are truly representative of Lassus's gifts, and not merely his smallest exercises, should therefore be studied if his greatness as a composer is to be fully recognized.

English music was at its zenith during the sixteenth century, the century of Shakespeare, whose plays abound in allusions to the power of music. In a number of memorable passages he asserts that music can change our very natures from the brutish to the sublime, and it was he who declared

> *That man that hath no music in himself,*
> *Nor is not moved with concord of sweet sounds,*
> *Is fit for treasons, stratagems, and spoils.*

During the latter part of the Middle Ages English composers such as John Dunstable (who died in 1453) had provided a type of musical leadership which continental composers gladly followed. For a considerable time, England was actually in the vanguard, musically speaking, rather than a mere follower as she became during the eighteenth and nineteenth centuries. The tradition of English musical excellence, moreover, continued throughout the entire Tudor period (1485–1603), and was revived fitfully during the seventeenth century. At least a score of English names will occur in any list of eminent sixteenth-century composers.

William Byrd (1543–1623), like Palestrina, Victoria and Lassus, appeared at a time when a hardy national school of composers flourished. Like them, he was fortunate enough to obtain early in life the support of powerful patrons. At the end of 1572 he was appointed organist of the Chapel Royal, a post which he shared with Thomas Tallis. The association of these two musicians first appeared in a licence dated January 22, 1575, in which Queen Elizabeth bestowed upon them both the exclusive right to print and sell music and music paper in England. Under this licence they produced in the same year a set of *Cantiones Sacrae* which they dedicated to the Queen. Each of the composers contributed seventeen motets to this publication, which was the first in England to be made up of Latin motets. Byrd's other patrons included eminent members of the nobility such as the Lord Chamberlain, Baron Hunsdon, Elizabeth's cousin, to whom he dedicated his *Songs of sundrie natures*, published in 1589. The dedication listed at length the favours bestowed upon him by Hunsdon (who was later to become one of Shakespeare's principal benefactors); he also recorded that 'since the publishing in print of my last labors in Musicke, diuers persons of great honor and worship have more esteemed & delighted in the exercise of that Art, then before.' His patrons followed the example set by Queen Elizabeth, who even in her old age continued to admire Byrd's music. The year before her death, according to a letter written on September 19th, 1602, by the Earl of Worcester, she still preserved her affection for a 'Lullaby', published some fourteen years before. Her constant favour was one of the composer's chief supports.

As a member of the Chapel Royal, Byrd had at his disposal one of the best choirs in the realm. He never underestimated the value of this opportunity for polished and correct interpretations of his work. He also realized that an important piece of music must be heard many times to appreciate its full value. Byrd asked 'all true lovers of Musicke' when listening to his compositions to

be but as carefull to heare them well expressed, as I haue

beene both in the Composing and correcting of them. Otherwise the best Song that euer was made will seeme harsh and vnpleasant, for that the well expressing of them, either by Voyces, or Instruments, is the life of our labours.

He then pointed out that any artistically made song

cannot be well perceiued nor vnderstood at the first hearing, but the oftener you shall heare it, the better cause of liking you shall discouer: and commonly that Song is best esteemed with which our eares are most acquainted.

As against Palestrina's 104, Lassus's 50, and Victoria's 21, Byrd wrote only three Masses. He was also less prolific as a composer of Latin motets than Palestrina or Lassus. He did, however, add considerably to Church music by using English texts, whereas the other three wrote no Church music with words in the language of their countries of origin. His English Church music consists principally of 'services' and anthems. The words of the 'services' come from the Book of Common Prayer. The anthems are settings of miscellaneous texts suited for singing in church, but not forming a part of the liturgy.

That for several centuries after Byrd's death only two of his anthems continued to be popular is due more to chance than to the nature of these compositions. In 1641 seven of these works were reprinted in a collection of 'church musick'. Between 1760 and 1778 Dr. William Boyce edited three volumes of another collection called *Cathedral Music* which contained only two of Byrd's anthems. These two anthems, quite arbitrarily chosen by Boyce, were sung in the latter part of the eighteenth and during the nineteenth century because they were easily available. But they were not, of course, truly representative of Byrd's talent. Musicians today recognize the haphazard ways in which certain 'samples' of the music of the past have survived while finer examples of a composer's work have been overlooked, and realize that often editorial whim rather than the considered judgment of Time is responsible.

Byrd has a further claim to fame above the other three for his keyboard music. A later chapter of this work, 'The Growth of Instrumental Virtuosity,' deals with his achievements as a composer for the virginals. And he explored yet other types of music untouched by the other three. He wrote incidental music for dramas. He supplied music for *Ricardus Tertius* (a Latin play on the same subject as Shakespeare's *Richard III*) of which a part survives. He anticipated Monteverdi with a type of dramatic solo song (string viol accompaniment) which even the great Italian composer, with his dramatic flair, could scarcely surpass. The song entitled 'Come Tread the Path' — thought to have been inserted into a love-tragedy entitled *Tancred and Gismunda* — gives some idea of Byrd's surprising dramatic powers.

Although more versatile than his three contemporaries, Byrd resembled them in so far as he wrote his greatest works in the same genre of serious choral music. As a composer of 'Motetts and Musicke of pietie and devotion' he has right of place beside the continental masters. One of the most discerning writers of the period, Henry Peacham, famous as both artist and author, said:

For Motetts and Musicke of pietie and devotion, as well as for the honour of our Nation, as the merit of the man,

I prefer above all . . . William Byrd, whom in that kind I know not whether any may equall, I am sure none excell, even by the judgment of France and Italy, who are very sparing in the commendation of strangers.

It is difficult to record sixteenth-century music, because music designed as a part of divine service tends to sound disappointing outside its proper setting. In a small listening space the hearer is apt to be unimpressed. Even the concert hall is scarcely the best place to hear it, and an 'effective' performance of, say, Byrd's motet *Ave Verum Corpus* (for 4 voices, from *Gradualia*, 1605) can hardly be thus rendered without distortion. Similarly, Victoria's expressive motets, *O quam gloriosum* and *O vos omnes*, famous examples from his first book of motets published in 1572, do not survive the impersonality of the auditorium. The right atmosphere seems to be rather the 'dim religious light' of *Il Penseroso*. Milton, indeed, has captured the feeling of this music:

> But let my due feet never fail
> To walk the studious cloister's pale,
> And love the high-embowèd roof,
> With antique pillars massy-proof,
> And storied windows richly dight,
> Casting a dim religious light.
> There let the pealing organ blow
> To the full-voiced choir below,
> In service high, and anthems clear,
> As may with sweetness, through mine ear,
> Dissolve me into ecstasies,
> And bring all Heaven before mine eyes.

In this passage he describes the prerequisites without which sixteenth-century polyphony sounds insipid, colourless, and flat. The long echoing and reechoing of the sound in a cathedral-like building transforms this music from a succession of colourless harmonies into a vibrant chain of sound.

The importance of resonance is perhaps more fully brought home by reference to the sound a piano makes when the damper pedal is not depressed. A Chopin Nocturne loses its fluency without a damper pedal to bind the harmonies together. It is the same with sixteenth-century polyphony. Between walls of stone the simplest triads reverberate and melt into each other in a way that is impossible in any other type of building, whereas on records, or over the air, this acoustical effect is usually lost. In the nave of a church sound reaches the ear from every direction; it is pin-pointed in the case of a record-player or wireless. If the 'service high, and anthems clear' of Byrd or any other sixteenth-century master are to dissolve us with their sweetness into the ecstasies Milton felt, then the music must be heard in its proper environment, or at least we must be able to re-create these ideal conditions.

The printed page of a sixteenth-century part-book tells us little about how a piece should be interpreted. Byrd's notation, for instance, does not indicate where to pitch the singers; what Byrd called C is not necessarily what we understand by this note. And his part-books contain almost no expression marks, just as Shakespeare's plays contained almost no indications of the techniques used in staging them at the Globe Theatre.

Because of the absence of expression marks analysis of the music tends to become dry and technical. Commentators who offer little more than dry statistics do not contribute to our appreciation of the music. Certainly our appetite for Byrd's, or his predecessor, John Taverner's music is not whetted by knowing the number of times 'false relations' occur.[1] A comparison of the number of *In Nomine* settings made by Byrd with those made by Taverner, Bull, or Tomkins, useful as it may be for the music historian, is of no assistance to the layman. We must be familiar with the music before its message becomes clear.

Vaughan Williams's *Fantasia on a Theme by Thomas Tallis* provides a useful introduction to Tudor spaciousness for the student who cannot hear sixteenth-century music performed adequately in suitable surroundings. This *Fantasia* for strings (violins, violas, 'cellos, and string basses) has a flavour of the past. *Fantasia* means a free wandering to and fro in which form is subservient to fancy, but in this composition Vaughan Williams follows the Tallis tune more closely than might be suspected at first hearing. The full-bodied string tone, moreover, has the same richness of sound as in Tallis's motet for forty voices entitled *Spem in alium*.

As supplementary reading Gustave Reese's *Music in the Renaissance* and *The New Oxford History of Music, Vol. IV*, are recommended. Reese's book is a standard work, and contains an exhaustive bibliography. *Grove's Dictionary of Music and Musicians, Fifth Edition*, contains authoritative lives of each composer mentioned in this chapter, together with lists of compositions.

[1] 'False relations' or cross-relations occur when two successive chords contain chromatically-related notes in *different* voice-parts, e.g. C in one chord in the soprano and C# in the next in the alto.

CHAPTER IV

SECULAR VOCAL MUSIC BEFORE 1600

Nowadays we classify a given piece of vocal music as 'secular' or 'sacred' by reference to the text. If the text is sacred we expect the music to be suitable for performance in church; if, on the other hand, the words are secular we expect it to be free from any such associations. The problem then is how to classify a piece of vocal music if in one manuscript the text is sacred, while in another of the same period the identical melody is joined to a profane text. Or, again, we may find a melody with double texts in the source manuscript, one secular and the other sacred. In a vocal composition it may happen that one voice is given a sacred text, while simultaneously another voice is directed to sing a lascivious love-song. These, and similar problems of classification, constantly arise when medieval 'secular' music comes to be analysed.

Among the oldest surviving pieces of medieval 'secular' music is one in a Cambridge manuscript which carries a bawdy text, O *admirabile Veneris ydolum*. But in another manuscript of equal antiquity, formerly in possession of the Benedictines at Monte Cassino, the same melody bears the words of a pilgrim song praising the Eternal City. Which is the earlier form, the sacred or the secular? On the basis of these two texts, in manuscripts of equal antiquity, it would seem that in the eleventh century, when the melody was composed, there was no sharp cleavage between 'sacred' and 'secular' styles.

The most famous of all medieval 'secular' compositions,

Sumer is icumen in, thought to have been written about 1240, poses a similar problem in classification. In the British Museum manuscript (Harleian 978) containing this delightful six-voice *rota*, the scribe wrote English words in one coloured ink expressing joy at the coming of summer and the singing of birds. Beneath the English words, however, he wrote in red ink Latin words, *Perspice Christicola*, which because of their piety any Reading monk could have sung between prime and compline. Is the composition sacred or secular? On manuscript evidence alone neither text could conclusively be proved to have preceded the other. Because of the buoyant lilt of the music, especially of the upper voices which dance about in the most carefree manner even though they are singing a rigorous canon,[1] scholars today assume that the secular text was the earlier. But the Reading monks, for whom John of Fornsete wrote the manuscript, can have felt no intrinsic enmity between the music and a sacred text, however much we today feel that the music departs from what we would like to believe is 'sacred' style.

When we come to examine the body of French motets written during 'the most glorious of all medieval centuries,' the thirteenth, we constantly encounter mixtures of texts, one voice singing an austere Gregorian melody with liturgical text at slow speed in an under part, while above, other voices disport themselves in frolicking love-songs. Are these motets sacred or secular? The answer can only be: a mixture of both. Certainly the medieval musician can have recognized no clearly marked division between

[1] The upper four voices follow each other in one 'circular' canon and the two lower in another. With further reference to canon, see note at bottom of p. 84.

'sacred' and 'secular' styles, if he could so blithely have accepted texts of both kinds.

It is only since the sixteenth century that a sharp division has been made between secular and sacred musical styles. Therefore it is not surprising to discover in the first large body of surviving secular music — the twelfth- and thirteenth-century melodies of the troubadours and trouvères — certain stylistic traits that strongly suggest the influence of contemporary liturgical music. The 264 troubadour and 1400 trouvère melodies which survive are written, if they show any rhythmic scheme, in notation which follows exactly the same system of time-values current in liturgical music of the period, 1100–1300. The structure of the troubadour and trouvère melodies, moreover, follows patterns already well known in liturgical music, such as the litany, the sequence, and the hymn. Attentive study of the repertory of troubadour and trouvère music has revealed that, although the aristocratic minstrels of the Age of Chivalry always prided themselves on writing 'original' melodies, their melodies were original only in details; in fundamental structure, all of them conform with certain familiar patterns found in Church music. Some scholars contend that the liturgical models upon which troubadour-trouvère music manifestly depended were in turn based on still older secular models, which have not survived. But this does not affect our main thesis. It is an indisputable fact that as far as musical style is concerned sacred and secular dwelt comfortably under the same roof during the Middle Ages.

The name of troubadour today suggests the romance of a Walter Scott novel. The troubadours slightly preceded the trouvères, and the primary distinction between them is one of geography — the troubadours coming from the south of France (Provence) and the trouvères from the north. Both groups were theoretically composed of nobility or royalty, Richard Cœur de Lion, for instance, counting himself a trouvère. A famous legend used by Sir Walter Scott describes how Richard was rescued from his Austrian dungeon by a trouvère who sang a melody known only to them both. Another king famous as a trouvère was Thibaut of Navarre (1201–1253), from whom 68 impassioned love-songs survive. But the most important of the trouvère composers was not a king. Adam de la Halle (1230?–1288?) was of obscure origin. He started life at Arras but later on was patronized by the French court at Naples, for which he wrote the music of a pastoral play, *Le Jeu de Robin et de Marion* (1285), sometimes listed in historical works as a prototype 'operetta'. Certain scholars have also claimed the incidental music for this play as our earliest source of folk-songs. Whether Adam de la Halle inserted folk-songs into the play or not, it is hardly likely that the trouvères as a group would have used melodies known to be the product of the lower classes.

Troubadour as well as trouvère music survives today only in the form of solo songs. As originally performed, however, it is thought that instrumental accompaniment was the rule. Where the rhythm of the melody is indicated in the manuscript sources, the modern time-equivalent is usually given as $\frac{3}{4}$ or $\frac{3}{8}$. The vocal range of the melodies rarely exceeds an octave, and no special virtuosic skill seems ever to have been required. The modes in which this music is cast include what we now call major and minor modes,[1]

[1] The word *mode* has another usage in connection with medieval music, referring not to the scale-system employed but rather to the rhythmic system. The six rhythmic modes of the thirteenth century all presupposed ternary metre.

in addition to a large proportion of Dorian and Mixo-lydian.

The subject-matter in most instances has to do with some aspect of courtly love, but the repertory also includes dance-songs, spinning-songs, military songs, and dramatic characterizations.

The German equivalents of the troubadours and trou-vères were known as Minnesinger, *Minne* meaning courtly love. The most renowned of the Minnesinger was Walther von der Vogelweide, immortalized in Wagner's opera *Tannhäuser* and his spirit re-created in *Die Meistersinger*. Walther's most famous melody, the 'Palestine Song' (1228), reminds us by its subject of the consuming interest in the Holy Land which then animated the crusading knights. Many of the German Minnelieder fall into the structural pattern: A_1 A_2 B. The first and second strophes use the same melodic strain, while the third departs from it into a new 'after-strain'. All are monodic — that is to say, solo songs. The usual interpretation today calls for a $\frac{3}{4}$ or $\frac{3}{8}$ time-signature, but much controversy has arisen over details of rhythmic transcription. Although both Dorian and Lydian modes are frequently found, Minnelieder only rarely cultivate the Mixolydian mode. Major and minor melodies are less frequently encountered than in the troubadour-trouvère repertory.

At the same time as the monodic secular music of the troubadours, trouvères, and Minnesinger, there developed in France, Italy, England, and to a lesser extent in Germany, several important types of polyphonic secular music. In France the leading secular composer during the fourteenth century was Guillaume de Machaut,[1] famous alike as poet,

[1] For Machaut's contribution to *Ars Nova* see p. 31.

cleric, adventurer, and musician. His secular music falls under these headings: 42 *ballades*, 33 *virelais* (=*chansons balladées*), 21 *rondeaux* and 18 *lais*. The formal scheme of his ballades may thus be diagrammed — *ab ab cd E*; and of his virelais (most of which are monodic rather than polyphonic) — *AB cc ab AB*. Each letter stands for a musical unit set off from other units by a cadence and a temporary relaxation of rhythmic movement; capital letters stand for musical units used as refrains. The structure of the music reflects the structure of the poetic text; cadences and rhythmic relaxation in the music are found where punctuation occurs in the text. For a proper appreciation the music should therefore be studied in conjunction with the text, more especially since Guillaume de Machaut, a poet of the first rank, often supplied his own. Needless to say, the subject-matter in his secular music is hardly the poetry one would expect from a priest. His poetry explores all the finer nuances of profane love. In style his secular and sacred music do not greatly differ, however opposite the sentiment expressed by the words. Both these types of music he endues with much the same learned and 'Gothic' features, such as isorhythm and imitation. What differences there are occur in the upper voices of his ballades and rondeaux where there is relatively more syncopation and elaborate embellishment. But no distinction is present regularly enough to permit classification of a piece as sacred or secular without reference to the accompanying text.

Italian music of the fourteenth century reflected more the spirit of the worldly and sensual Boccaccio than the spiritual and ascetic Dante. The leading composers, Jacopo da Bologna (*ca.* 1350) and Francesco Landini (1325-1397), both wrote excellent madrigals. It is thought that the word madrigal is derived from *matricale*, meaning 'in the mother tongue'. As an art for the sophisticated upper classes the madrigals of Jacopo da Bologna and Landini bore some resemblance to those of the sixteenth century, which were also enjoyed by the élite. But stylistically, the fourteenth- and sixteenth-century madrigal differed radically. (As in the case of the word 'motet', 'madrigal' so changed its meaning in two hundred years that no secure musical connection can now be established between earlier and later usages.)

The most popular international secular type of music during the fifteenth century was the *chanson*. In its generic sense, '*chanson*' means, of course, nothing more than song. To fix more exactly the stages of its development it is now usual to speak of fifteenth-century *chanson* as 'Burgundian *chanson*', because the most accomplished composers of this period — Guillaume Dufay (1400?–1474) and Gilles Binchois (1400?–1460)[1] — were Burgundians.

The following general observations may be made on the Burgundian *chanson*: (1) The majority were written for three voices, with the lower being tenor and contratenor; (2) for melodic interest the top voice always predominates; (3) instrumental support is usually presumed, and long vocal passages are often preceded, interspersed, and followed by short instrumental sections; (4) as a rule, fifteenth-century *chansons* are strophic, the same music doing duty for several stanzas; (5) the rhythms are always incisive, and there is often a carol-like atmosphere; (6) the subject-matter of the poetry concerns *materiae amatoriae* — love themes — to use the words of Johannes Tinctoris, who de-

---

[1] Throughout this chapter dates of composers' lives can often be only approximate.

fined the *chanson* in his 1475 musical dictionary, *Terminorum musicae diffinitorium* (published at Naples).

The pattern of the poetry frequently follows this plan (each small letter in the diagram below standing for a couplet):

I	II	III	Conclusion
a	c	d	a
b	a	e	

The concluding couplet, whose text is identical with the opening couplet, acts as a refrain, and music as well as words are repeated, thus producing a rounded form.

In Dufay's *chansons* imitation is frequently used as a unifying device. By imitation is meant the entrance of one voice with a melody, which is then taken up by the other voices in turn and woven into a rich fabric of independently moving parts. Imitation most frequently occurs in lively and gay *chansons* like *Ce jour de l'an*. In more reflective and pensive *chansons* such as *Se la face ay pale*, Dufay tends to write harmony in solid blocks (vertical harmony).

In a song where a tenor voice sings in Latin a scriptural text such as 'From whence cometh my help', while the top voice sings in French, 'I can do no more than I have already done, I can be no other than I am', we can see how the Burgundian *chanson* is linked with the past. The highly schematic plan of the older Gothic music intrudes occasionally when a tenor voice repeats a musical passage three times: each repeat being twice as fast as the one preceding it.

In the hands of Dufay, its principal exponent, the Burgundian *chanson* expresses the most tender and gracious sentiments. Let us analyse his *chanson*, *Se la face ay pale*, written for three parts, a vocal duet and an instrumental 'contratenor'. The text of this *chanson* is in three stanzas of ten short lines with two feet to the line, the tenth line in each stanza acting as a refrain. The music reflects the poetic structure. Lines 1, 3 and 8 are matched with slow opening chords which then dissolve into fast motion. The four principal cadences are: plagal, authentic, a half-cadence, and authentic. These cadences, which perfectly match the poetic structure, mark off the successive stages of self-revelation as the lover tells his woe and reveals the reasons for his pale, wan, and woe-begone countenance. Moreover, this *chanson*, which is clearly in C Major, is homophonic throughout. Dufay's fondness for this particular *chanson* is shown by his later use of it in one of his finest Masses of the 'parody' type, a Mass not only generated from the *chanson* but also entitled *Se la face ay pale*.[1]

Following the example of the English musician, mathematician and astrologer, John Dunstable (canon of Hereford Cathedral, retainer of the Duke of Bedford, and on the Continent the acknowledged mentor of an entire generation in the then new art of polyphony), Dufay strove not only for a fuller sonority (the filling up of the chords so that all three notes in a triad appear) but was also one of the earliest composers to study chord-progression. Whereas a century earlier Machaut in his secular music merely added line to line, Dufay conceived all his voice-parts as an integral whole. Perhaps we may be permitted a somewhat homely analogy in our effort to make the distinction clear. Machaut had assembled his confections like an ice-cream manufacturer who adds a layer of chocolate to a layer of

---

[1] When used in connection with fifteenth- and sixteenth-century Masses 'parody' does not mean a caricature or a 'take-off', but that a previously existing composition becomes the basis of a newly-composed Mass.

vanilla, followed by a layer of strawberry. Each layer, however, tastes quite as well by itself, or in conjunction with only one other layer. With Dufay, however, the layers are no longer separately manufactured. They are brought into being simultaneously, and can no more be separated after manufacture than tutti-frutti ice-cream can be broken down into its individual ingredients.

At the opening of the sixteenth century the *chanson* still had international ascendancy over other types of secular music. The principal composers, however, were no longer Burgundians but Flemings. Among the masters represented in the *chanson* collections published shortly after 1500 by Ottaviano de' Petrucci, the first great music printer, we find Josquin des Prez (1450?–1521), Alexander Agricola (1446?–1506), Antoine Busnois and Philippe Caron. The sixteenth-century *chanson* as cultivated in France provides a remarkable number of examples. To name only one publisher, Pierre Attaignant of Paris, we find that more than 1500 *chansons* were printed in his collections (1528–1562).

As might be expected, the subject-matter in so large a literature was extremely varied. War, the hunt, weddings, and drinking all had their place, but variants of the love theme predominated. And it was not only the pleasure-loving classes who enjoyed these lively *chansons*; they were even favoured by the severe Huguenots. For the sake of decorum, however, the Huguenots changed the words and reissued *chanson*-collections with new, more edifying texts, which they then called *chansons spirituelles*.[1]

The *chanson*, which during its Burgundian phase was primarily 3-voice, became 4-voice in its Flemish phase

[1] For an example, see p. 50.

(*ca.* 1500); later during the sixteenth century 5 voices became the common number and *chansons* for as many as 6, 7, and 8 voices were frequently written. The form reached its highest point of perfection in the hands of the French masters Clément Jannequin (1485?–1560) and Claude de Sermisy [Claudin] (1490?–1562). Jannequin specialized in descriptive *chansons* bearing such titles as *La Bataille* (describing in lively fashion the Battle of Marignano of 1515), *La Prise de Boulogne* ('The Capture of Boulogne'), *La Chasse* ('The Stag-Hunt'), *Le Caquet des femmes* ('The Prattle of Women'), and *Le Chant des Oiseaux* ('The Song of the Birds'). Claudin's *chansons*, although not usually bearing such picturesque titles, are more varied in emotional content.

Because of its strong rhythm the sixteenth-century French *chanson* was eminently suitable for instrumental accompaniment. The voice-parts contain many repeated notes as well as recurrent short, pungent, rhythmic figures. In transcription for spinet or harpsichord, and more especially in arrangement for lute, the *chanson* lost none of its effectiveness. There were so few long sustained notes in the voice-parts that plucked instruments could perfectly take the place of voices in a transcribed version.

The sixteenth-century *chanson* had clear-cut sections. Punctuation in the text was reflected by clear cadences in the voice-parts and often the same music did duty for successive stanzas. The use of such older Gregorian modes as the Dorian and Phrygian, which had already begun to go out of fashion in the Burgundian *chanson*, was almost completely rejected in the sixteenth century. Modern major and minor took their place.

Melody tended at all times to give way to rhythm. An

extreme instance of concentration on rhythmic problems is found in the so-called *chansonnettes mesurées*, first published in 1586 by Jacques Mauduit and Claude Le Jeune. In these 'measured' *chansons* the metre of the verse dictated the rhythm of the music. If the verse was dactylic the music usually followed a pattern of minims (half-notes) plus two crotchets (quarter-notes); if iambic it fell into ternary rhythm with an upbeat followed by a note lasting two beats. The French humanist scholars were partly responsible for this curious attempt to write music according to foot-rule. Structurally, however, French is far removed from Greek or Latin, and in determining rhythm in French poetry stress on accented syllables counts for more than vowel-lengths found in classical Latin. The passage of twenty years saw an end to the experiment in *vers mesuré* and with it the *chanson mesurée*.

To summarize, the sixteenth-century *chanson* exhibited the following features: (1) polyphonic and homophonic sections frequently alternated; (2) formal devices, such as imitation, were used but never in a ponderous way; (3) the sections within a *chanson* were always clearly set off from each other by cadences; (4) cadences were placed where punctuation occurred in the text; (5) rhythmic interest obtained by repeated notes and repeated rhythmic figures ('*ostinato* figures') tended to overshadow purely melodic considerations; (6) the sonorous ideal was conceived in terms of voices plus instruments, rather than voices alone.

After 1530 the Italian madrigal became the other principal secular musical form. But while the *chanson* retained wide popularity throughout the century the Italian madrigal had a more restricted appeal. For the most part it was appreciated by the higher levels of society. Even in England, where it became popular after 1588, there is ample evidence that madrigal-singing was practiced by the élite, and not by the middle classes.

The predecessor, though not the parent, of the madrigal was the *frottola*. The word *frottola*, once thought to be a derivative of *frutta*, fruit, is now considered to have come from *frocta*, meaning a medley of heterogeneous ideas. The *frottola*, which as a musical form originated shortly before 1500, was an attempt by native Italian composers to oppose the international art-forms practised by such Flemish masters resident in Italy as Josquin des Prez and Heinrich Isaac.

The literature of the *frottola* contained the kind of erotica every young gallant at a Renaissance court in Italy needed for his assault upon fair ladies. The words were often obscene, and the music deliberately obvious and superficial. The principal melody was always assigned to the top voice. The bass was usually little more than an accompaniment for the upper voices. Taken alone his part contained nothing of interest. The inner voices were only fillers. There was nothing subtle about the *frottola*. Though, unlike the *villanella* (another kind of Italian song), it did not cultivate the country-bumpkin type of false harmony, it was nevertheless often both banal and repetitious.

In his authoritative study, *The Italian Madrigal*, Einstein says that this form of part-song 'originated in the disintegration of the *frottola*, more exactly, a disintegration for the sake of expression' (I, 119). The madrigal eschewed the rhythmic squareness of the *frottola* with its everlasting 'bump' of the cadences at the ends of phrases, replacing squareness with suppleness, simple homophony with a polyphonic texture in which each voice shared equal melodic honours. Almost invariably the music was composed straight through, without calling upon the opening section to do duty for second and third stanzas as well. Instead of the few restricted harmonic 'formulas' used by composers of the *frottola*, the harmonic patterns of the madrigalists were infinitely varied. Although Gregorian modes were not systematically used they did influence the work of the madrigalists. The sonorous ideal was an unaccompanied vocal music in which each voice part was sung by a soloist. Thus a 5-voice madrigal implied five solo singers, no more, no less, who sang without lute or other accompaniment. Five-voice texture was the most frequent at mid-century, but 4-voice and 6-voice textures were also common. Except at their inception, when Costanzo Festa (1490?–1545) wrote them, madrigals for 3 voices were unknown.

The madrigal, because it quickly assumed pride of place in secular music, was taken up even by the most serious ecclesiastical composers. Palestrina, while he wrote madrigals, never wrote villanelle, villote, mascherate, or any of the other popular types comprised loosely under the term *canti carnascialeschi* (carnival songs), because it would not have been thought seemly. When dedicating one of his works to the Pope he professed himself too serious-minded even for madrigal-writing.[1] But when he did descend to writing madrigals the result was not unworthy of his great name. Serious ecclesiastical composers could write madrigals because they were able to use, though to a lesser extent, the same subtleties and artifices that were considered appropriate to the exalted music of the Church.

[1] Compare p. 50.

The emergence of the madrigal as a sixteenth-century art-form can be traced with satisfying precision to the year 1530. It was then that the first collection with the word 'madrigal' in its title was printed.[1]

The three masters of the madrigal in its earliest period were Philippe Verdelot (1480?-1539?), Costanzo Festa (1490?-1545), and Jacques Arcadelt (1504?-1567?). Verdelot, chapel-master at Venice and Florence, and Arcadelt, singer in the papal choir at Rome, were both French. Of particular significance is the number of composers writing madrigals in the sixteenth century who were Italian only by adoption. This predominance of foreigners — Frenchmen and Flemings — was more or less fortuitous. In the fifteenth century they had been the chief exponents of Italian music. By the end of the next century Italian composers had completely ousted them. During this period (1500-1600) these foreign composers only held on in Italy by becoming more Italian than the Italians themselves.

Adrian Willaert (1490?-1562) in the first generation, and Philippe de Monte (1521-1603), Orlandus Lassus (1532?-1594), and Giaches de Wert (1536-1596) in the second, provide examples of Flemings who either in or outside Italy competed with the foremost Italian composers of their time in the production of madrigals. In particular, Philippe de Monte, who met Thomas Tallis in London in 1555 and later corresponded with William Byrd, and who spent his last thirty-five years in Vienna and Prague, wrote more madrigals than any Italian or any other non-Italian composer.

[1] Musically speaking, the madrigal of the fourteenth century (Jacopo da Bologna and Francesco Landini) cannot claim to be the progenitor of the sixteenth-century madrigal.

In 1569 a prominent Italian composer of madrigals made the following summary of his task: 'The notes are the body of the music, but the text is the soul. Just as the soul, being nobler than the body, must be followed and imitated by it, so the notes must follow the text and imitate it. The composer must always pay it its due attention, expressing its sense with sad, gay, or austere music, as the text demands.' The motto of every madrigal composer might well have been: 'Music, the servant of the Italian language.'

The text so completely dictated its musical clothing that when in a madrigal a word such as 'darkness' occurred the composer immediately wrote down a series of black notes. The word 'descend' was symbolised by a downward slope in the musical line and conversely the line sloped upward for the word 'ascend'. If the word 'eyes' occurred in the text, then adjacent semibreves (whole-notes) were used, because on paper they looked like eyes. Visually descriptive notation was carried to such lengths by some composers that words such as 'heart' and 'leaf' were illustrated by arrangement of the musical lines.

This concern for the visual arose from the fact that the madrigal was an art for performers, not for auditors. Madrigal-singing was a courtly pastime, and as long as the musical education of a courtier included sight-reading and the ability to carry his part against other moving solo voices, the madrigal flourished. As soon as the courtier ceased to take part in sight-reading and was content to listen to others, the art died. In its heyday madrigal-singing was the favourite diversion at supper parties. Because the majority of madrigals treated of woman and her charms, the pleasures of song were often a prelude to those of the flesh. During the earliest period (1530–1550), parts for male voices generally predominated; in the second generation (after 1550), men and women singers were on an equal footing.

The high regard for Italian culture is reflected in the popularity of the madrigal outside Italy. Monte in Prague continued to write madrigals as prolifically as he had done when living in Naples and Florence. Lassus was still writing them thirty years after moving to Munich. Wherever one turns, whether to Spain, England, or Germany, there is evidence of Italian hegemony. In Spain the two Mateo Flechas, Pedro Ruimonte (who worked, however, in Belgium), and Joan Brudieu wrote madrigals. Transcriptions of madrigals by Rodrigo Ceballos, Francisco Guerrero (1528–1599), Juan Navarro, and Pedro Ordoñez are reported in the *Libro de música en cifras para Vihuela, intitulado El Parnasso* (1576), published by Esteban Daza at Valladolid. In England, beginning a little later with Nicholas Yonge's *Musica Transalpina* (1588), we find a spate of publications devoted to madrigals in their original tongue, in English translation and adaptation. Even so 'English' a composer as Thomas Morley (1557–1603) published his madrigals simultaneously in two editions, one with Italian and the other with English texts.

The history of the madrigal in the country of its origin shows three successive stages: (1) early madrigal (1530–1550), predominantly for 4 voices; the three composers Verdelot, Arcadelt, and Festa wrote in a deliberately 'Arcadian' style, exploring delicate and graceful emotions; (2) the mature madrigal (1550–1580), predominantly for 5 voices; the masters Willaert, Cipriano de Rore, Palestrina, Lassus, and Monte undertook texts with a deeper note of pathos, often writing in the taut and concentrated 'imitative' manner considered appropriate for motets, with rare homophonic passages; (3) late madrigal (1580–1620), showing a tendency towards mannerism; the principal masters, Luca Marenzio (1553–1599), Carlo Gesualdo, Prince of Venosa (1560–1615), and Claudio Monteverdi (1567–1643), chose texts which reached out to the uttermost confines of human emotion, and their music followed suit with extreme harmonic audacities and rhythmic complexities, in order to express the violence of the texts. In this last period the madrigal-composers inhabited a world made colourful for English readers in such poetry as Browning's *My Last Duchess* and Shelley's *Cenci*. In its third phase the madrigal discarded the niceties of *a cappella* singing, and moved into the domain of solo song with accompaniment. The logical successor of the expiring madrigal was the Baroque solo aria with instrumental accompaniment.

The madrigal, for all purposes, died a natural death when (1) an ensemble of solo singers, each with equal rights and privileges, gave way to one dominant solo singer accompanied by either other voices or instruments; (2) the Italian upper social classes no longer considered sight-singing ability the necessary equipment of a man of parts; (3) musical skills became professionalized so that only a highly trained singer dared offer himself as a public performer. The madrigals published after 1640 were all deliberate archaisms. The last of the Spenserian tributes to a vanished past probably appeared in 1705, when Antonio Lotti, *maestro di cappella* at St. Mark's, Venice, published his *Duetti, Terzetti, Madrigali*.[1]

---

[1] From this collection Handel's rival, Bononcini, stole a madrigal; his downfall followed the exposure of his theft.

In England the last madrigal to be published appeared shortly before the accession of Charles I. The glory of English madrigal, as shown in the work of such consummate masters as John Wilbye (*First Set of Madrigals*, 1598; *Second Set*, 1609) and Thomas Weelkes (*Madrigals of 5 parts*, 1600; *Madrigals of 6 parts*, 1600), was all too short-lived. In the hands of such men as Morley, George Kirbye, Francis Pilkington, and Robert Jones, not to mention Wilbye and Weelkes and the profound and masterly Orlando Gibbons (1583–1625), the English madrigal was no mere epigonous salute to Italian culture. Just as Shakespeare adapted from Giraldi Cinthio and Bandello, or Beaumont and Fletcher from Ariosto and Tasso, so the English madrigalists in the process of adapting often strengthened the very material which they imitated. No better example perhaps can be cited than that of the English madrigalists to prove that the infiltration of a foreign musical culture can actually stimulate rather than stultify native genius.

As supplementary reading, in addition to the books listed at the end of the preceding chapter, the student is referred to Alfred Einstein's definitive study in three volumes, *The Italian Madrigal*, and to E. H. Fellowes' *The English Madrigal Composers*.

CHAPTER V

THE RISE OF OPERA

Opera, that is to say sung drama, made its first appearance in Florence. It was started by an aristocratic group known as the Camerata which did not, however, regard it as a new art-form but merely as a return to the musical methods of classic Greek drama.

Aristotle believed that tragedy, the most ennobling form of drama, should be written in poetry enhanced in some parts with melody, but in others recited without singing. The language of tragedy, he said, should be 'embellished and rendered pleasurable'. The means of embellishing and rendering pleasurable included in his opinion melody and poetic metre. He added, however, that 'in some parts metre alone is employed, in others, melody'. The Florentines who assembled at the sumptuous residence of Count Giovanni Bardi took Aristotle's dicta to mean that in classic Greek drama all the lines were sung.

An outspoken member of the Camerata, Vincenzo Galilei (father of the celebrated astronomer, Galileo Galilei), advocated in his *Dialogue of Ancient and Modern Music* (1581) the abandonment of all the devices of polyphony and a return to the pristine simplicity of ancient Greek music. Galilei was unable to transcribe into comprehensible music notation any of the three ancient Greek hymns included as examples in his *Dialogue*, but carried away by an ardent enthusiasm for the vanished glories of ancient Greece he, like another musical enthusiast of the same century, Nicola Vicentino, vainly imagined that the

79

musical art of the Periclean age could be restored. This same spirit of enthusiasm inspired the other members of the Camerata. To recapture what they conceived to be the original practice of the ancients, they swept aside in one grandiose gesture the 'tiresome intricacies' of sixteenth-century polyphony, and forthwith declared war on counterpoint.

In their enthusiasm for antiquity they committed themselves to a stylized type of declamation now known as Florentine monody, which implied a simple voice line supported by only the thinnest of accompaniments. The singer, however, did declaim his lines so that every word could be clearly understood. This was essential since the meaning of the words was more important than the beauty of the melody. Jacopo Peri (1561–1633), composer of the first opera (*Dafne*, 1597), justified the subordination of melody to achieve an understandable text in the following passage:

> I believe that the ancient Greeks and Romans (who, according to the opinion of many, sang their tragedies throughout) used a kind of music more advanced than ordinary speech, but less than the melody of singing, thus taking a middle position between the two.

The music of Peri's *Dafne* is now lost, but that of another of his operas, *Euridice* (1600), has survived, showing his methods. The words are at all times understandable; no such strictly musical consideration as a search for variety in the types of cadences deters Peri from allowing text pride of place. Though *Euridice* contains ten scenes, nowhere is music used to fill in background; there are no instrumental interludes between any of the scenes, and the occasional choruses alternating with the almost continuous solo declamation eschew any of the richnesses of polyphony.

The author of the words in both *Dafne* and *Euridice* was the skilful poet, Ottavio Rinuccini (1562–1621). The words of *Euridice* (the 'libretto') were set to music not only by Peri, but also by another member of the Camerata, Giulio Caccini (1546–1618). Caccini's setting, however, differs only slightly from Peri's, since both were obsessed with the same idea that text was all-important.

In the same way that Watling Island, the first land Columbus touched in the New World, would never be mentioned in history texts had not he and his successors returned to discover the two Americas, so, but for the achievements of Monteverdi and other opera composers of his stature, Caccini's or Peri's *Euridice* would never be mentioned in present-day histories of music. The course of operatic history before Monteverdi can be summarized under three headings: (1) its birth was attended by a group of Florentine aristocrats whose imperfect knowledge of Greek drama led them to imagine that they were restoring ancient practice; (2) the subject-matter of the earliest operas was drawn from Greek and Roman mythology; (3) the audiences were composed of wealthy aristocrats, and the earliest presentations of opera took place in the private mansions of influential people who expected to be flattered directly or indirectly in the texts. (*Euridice*, for instance, began with a Prologue complimenting the 'noble auditors'.)

Claudio Monteverdi (1567–1643) was a much more highly trained musician than either Peri or Caccini. The rejection of counterpoint by Peri and Caccini may have been just as much the amateur's disdain of a subject he cannot master as the revolutionary's contempt for the stodgy and outmoded. But Monteverdi was professionally competent. He was trained under Marc' Antonio Ingegneri, whose Responses for Holy Week were for a long time erroneously attributed to Palestrina. Throughout his long career, which extended through almost half the seventeenth century, Monteverdi rarely indulged his tendencies towards revolutionary writing in any of his sacred choral works,[1] and never when writing for *a cappella* chorus. Rather he preferred to write in the noble ecclesiastical style of the sixteenth century. Judged solely by his Church music, then, Monteverdi, although he must be recognized as a master, can hardly be said to have broken new ground.

In the writing of madrigals (he published five books before composing his first opera), Monteverdi also showed his debt to the past; not so much to Ingegneri (on the title-page of Book I [1587] he described himself as his disciple) but rather to Cipriano de Rore, the master of the so-called chromatic style in this form of music. Both in his Masses and madrigals Monteverdi showed his indebtedness to the sixteenth century. His madrigals, though superb, are not finer than those of Luca Marenzio; and his Masses do not surpass those of Palestrina. But as an opera composer during the first half of the seventeenth century he had no peer.

His first opera, *Orfeo* (1607), the music of which fortunately survives, has so much vitality that it has been suc-

---

[1] His 1610 *Vespers* (from which the *Magnificat* performed at the 1953 Three Choirs Festival was taken) shows him in one of his most dramatic moods, and contrasts strongly with the great bulk of his ecclesiastical mus .

cessfully revived several times during this century. In sharp
contrast to Peri's pale *Euridice* which only required four
instruments, thirty-six are specified in the score to *Orfeo*.
Whereas in Caccini's and Peri's *Euridice* there were no
instrumental numbers, in *Orfeo* Monteverdi introduced
twenty-six individual movements for instrumental ensemble. In *Orfeo* Monteverdi used notable devices to
achieve a larger unity within the opera; in both *Euridices*
no devices were employed to unite the ten individual
scenes. The repetition of short refrain-like passages were
among the devices used by Monteverdi to give his operas
the appearance of a cohesive whole. The opening Ritor-
nello, for instance, is repeated several times in the opera:
first at the end of the Prologue, then at the end of Acts II
and IV. Similarly the short passage called 'Symphony' (not,
of course, in the present-day sense) which Monteverdi used
at the end of Act II appears again later in a modified form.
The Symphony at the beginning of Act III is also heard
again in Act V.

The instruments were divided into categories; various
emotions were represented by different instrumental
groups. Each emotion therefore evoked from the orchestra
its own individual tone-colouring. In the accompaniment,
certain chords were repeated as, for instance, where a Messenger tells Orpheus of his wife's death, the Messenger
being represented by the E major chord, and the stunned
Orpheus by the dramatically contrasting key of G minor.
The emotions of the actors in the drama were underlined
by other appropriate musical means such as dramatic chord
changes, individualized accompaniments, and contrasts in
the types of melody assigned to the different singers.

Orfeo is therefore architecturally satisfying; the inner

cohesion in all its parts is admirable. Monteverdi, in showing concern for unity of impression throughout the work, while at the same time endowing each part with appropriately individualized music, succeeded in creating a wholly satisfying masterpiece. His choruses, in contrast with those of Peri and Caccini, did not neglect the devices of counterpoint. Rather they used all its resources. Even in the solo airs for the principal singers the composer occasionally introduced counter-melodies. In the apotheosis at the end, for instance, canon[1] is introduced. Apollo in the act of translating Orpheus from this too harsh world into the less perturbed regions of Heaven, sings with Orpheus a duet in canon. This strict contrapuntal device would undoubtedly have been anathema to Peri and his fellow Florentines.

The story of Orpheus in classical mythology had an unhappy ending, but unhappy endings were unpopular in early opera. The myth as Monteverdi used it told the story of Eurydice's death and of Orpheus's search for her in the underworld. By his music Orpheus softened the heart of Pluto, who allowed Eurydice to return with him to earth provided he did not look back until he reached the upper world. Orpheus doubted Pluto's promise and looked back. In the classic myth he then lost Eurydice for ever, but in Monteverdi's opera Apollo took pity and carried him to celestial regions. At the end of Monteverdi's opera a chorus and ballet express joy and happiness at Orpheus's ascent to Heaven.

Orfeo was commissioned by Vincenzo Gonzaga, Duke of Mantua, a patron whom Monteverdi served as chapel-

---

[1] Canon is the coupling of voices which sing the same melody, but with one voice starting ahead of the other.

master from 1602 to 1612. The Mantuan ducal family had already established a tradition of musical patronage: Guglielmo, the father of Monteverdi's patron, had given Palestrina financial support. Palestrina did not go to live in Mantua, but other well-known musicians had lived there, and its musical tradition was strong. Monteverdi, moreover, had in Vincenzo a patron who had an enlightened taste in musical matters. The wedding celebrations in 1600 of the duke's sister-in-law, who later became Queen of France, provided the occasion for the first performance of *Euridice*. The Mantuans prided themselves on keeping abreast of the newest musical developments, and only after Vincenzo's death did Monteverdi go elsewhere.

The one other opera composed by Monteverdi in Mantua which deserves notice was *Arianna*. Its music, with the exception of a celebrated lament, has (like Peri's *Dafne* of 1597) unfortunately been lost. The plot, like that of *Dafne*, *Orfeo*, and *Euridice*, was drawn from mythology; the libretto was by the same aristocratic Rinuccini who wrote the words of *Euridice*. The first performance of *Arianna* in the Mantuan ducal palace on the occasion of an important family marriage is said to have attracted the leading nobility from all over Italy.

The Ariadne story tells of a deserted wife. At the first performance the singer who took the part 'told her cruel torments and drew a thousand tears from a thousand breasts'. All that now remains of the opera is the 'Lamento'. Monteverdi's own wife had died only a few months before, and his profound grief seems to have been poured into his Lament. Realizing its poignant passion, he himself prized it above all his compositions, and later arranged it first as a five-part madrigal, and then, provided with sacred words, as the five-part *Pianto della Madonna* (1640). Some of his admirers reproached him for 'thus having disfigured the pearl of his compositions', but others welcomed these arrangements as a means of making his name more widely known.

Few compositions have so profoundly expressed an overwhelming sense of loss and grief. Like other Italians who attributed particular powers to the Greek philosophers, Monteverdi attributed to Plato his power of expression in the Lament. A quarter of a century after writing it he explained the source of his inspiration.

> When I was about to compose the Lament of Ariadne, I could find no book which could enlighten me on natural methods of imitation, or which would even authorize me to imitate, save Plato; and he in a manner so obscure, that, with my feeble comprehension, I could scarcely comprehend the little which he revealed.

The Lament as Monteverdi originally conceived it was accompanied by the subdued music of viols; the orchestra throughout *Arianna*, moreover, is known to have been placed out of sight behind the stage. When, in the nineteenth century, Wagner had the orchestra in the Bayreuth Festival Opera House concealed, he was only repeating what Monteverdi had done more than two centuries earlier.

Monteverdi spent the last thirty years of his life in Venice as Master of Music of the Most Serene Republic and *maestro di cappella* at St. Mark's. There he worthily upheld traditions established by such masters as Adrian Willaert and the two Gabrielis, Andrea and Giovanni, uncle and nephew. His operas which survive from the Venetian period were both written after the opening of the first public opera house, the Teatro San Cassiano, in 1637. (This opening was an important event in operatic history, for henceforth opera, though still the diversion of kings and princes, was available, in Venice at least, to all who could pay the subscription price.) In the second of Monteverdi's surviving Venetian operas, *L'Incoronazione di Poppea* ('The Coronation of Poppaea'), he departed, for the first time, from mythological themes and used instead an historical subject; the story concerns the Emperor Nero's infatuation with the wife of one of his generals. This story, a variant on the David-Bathsheba tale, provided Monteverdi with an opportunity to delineate human emotions at their most primitive, and the music is one of the great achievements of the seventeenth century.

Later seventeenth-century Venetian composers wrote operas in which spectacular scenic effects were procured by the use of stage machinery. Tempests, battles, incantations, thrilling rescues by divine interposition, gurgling fountains, dragons spouting torrents of flame, birds singing in gardens, thunder, lightning, wind, rain, were all reproduced. The plots now seem for the most part ineffectual and somewhat absurd. The principal singers were often *castrati*, whose boyish voices had been preserved and their vocal range increased by castration at the age of twelve or thereabouts. These eunuchs were paid fabulous salaries and received the adulation now accorded to film stars. In Venetian opera, choruses were seldom used because the public demanded stars, not choruses; and stars they had, male, female, and eunuch. As opera in Venice and elsewhere became commercialized, artistic standards declined, and there was little musical merit in the typical late baroque opera.

In France, Germany and Austria, Italian influence determined the main trends in opera history during the seventeenth century. Although in England the influence of Italy was at first felt somewhat indirectly, the indebtedness of Purcell's masterpiece, *Dido and Aeneas*, to Italian cantata models can be shown. In his introduction to *Dioclesian* Purcell called the Italians the 'best masters' for English composers to follow. It can justly be said, therefore, that opera wherever it grew owned Italy as its parent.

The two most prominent figures in French opera during the period of the *ancien régime* were Jean-Baptiste Lully (1632–1687) and Jean-Philippe Rameau (1683–1764). Lully, a Florentine by birth, arrived in Paris at the age of fourteen when Cardinal Mazarin, an Italian himself, was the real ruler of France during the minority of Louis XIV. He started in a humble capacity as a violinist and dancer, but soon attracted the attention of the young king, who made him composer of the royal chamber music. His rise to fame was due not only to his undoubted musical gifts, but also to his success as a courtier who knew how to please Louis XIV's every whim. He was ruthless towards potential competitors, and extremely grasping and arrogant. Though himself an Italian he intrigued against other Italians in France by professing a desire for a distinctively French style in opera.

It was Lully who first wrote the type of introductory movement known as a 'French overture'. He also developed a style of musical declamation peculiarly suited to the French language. His choice of texts showed literary discrimination, and his refined technique in adjusting music to words was much admired.

His 'French overture' was widely copied by other composers; the introductory movement began with a slow, pompous section in which the principal beats were preceded by a short pick-up note or group of pick-up notes. These notes, occurring just before the principal beats, when executed with great force and precision undoubtedly gave the rhythm a remarkable vitality. After the opening passage the strings would break into a lively 'fugal' section[1] in $\frac{3}{8}$ or $\frac{6}{8}$ metre with themes constantly bandied to and fro. At the end of this lively section in imitative style there was occasionally a repeat (in somewhat abbreviated form) of the opening stately section. The French overture can be said to have perfectly expressed in musical terms the pride and arrogance of the French court.

Of Lully's seventeen dramatic works eleven were 'lyrical tragedies' based on classical subjects and another pair were _tragédies_ founded on medieval romances. His opera plots centred on conflicts between love and duty, and the principal characters were thinly disguised representations of important contemporaries. Because he dedicated himself to the one task of pleasing the King and the court, he reaped the reward of immediate and overwhelming success during his lifetime. He always showed himself as sensitive as a weather-vane to shifts in the political wind, and his ability to accommodate himself to every change in the political climate proved an ever-useful asset. He thereby not only dominated the French musical scene but amassed

---

[1] The term 'fugue' is discussed at p. 149. The fast sections in French overtures start in the manner of a fugue, but after the 'exposition' collapse into sequences and loose imitation.

G

a huge fortune. Although a part was derived from shrewd speculation in landed property, the bulk of his enormous estate represented money made directly in musical enterprises of one kind and another. He died at the height of his musical powers, at fifty-five, and his last work, *Acis et Galathée*, is a masterpiece of lightness, youthful sparkle, and verve.

Lully carefully distinguished between styles suitable for the theatre and those suitable for the church. When he heard an arrangement of one of his airs sung in church he was incensed and called the singer to account. (His sound commercial instinct probably informed him that he was making no money out of an arrangement for church purposes.) He did not, however, completely neglect sacred composition. His *Miserere*, written in about his thirtieth year (1664), stands as one of the greatest monuments of his art. In it he showed himself a master of contrapuntal writing, and his contrasting of soloists, double chorus, and full orchestra was admirably handled. Madame de Sévigné said of this work, 'I do not believe the heavenly choirs themselves sing any finer music.'

Jean-Philippe Rameau (1683–1764) made his reputation not in opera, but rather as a writer on theoretical subjects. He composed his first opera when he was fifty. *Hippolyte et Aricie* (1733), a masterly work, was followed by the equally noteworthy operas, *Castor et Pollux* (1737) and *Dardanus* (1739). His librettos were poor, however, and he seems not to have cared what kind of words he set. (As Voltaire, his contemporary, once said: 'What is too silly to be said is sung.')

Like Lully, Rameau considered ballet an integral part

of his operas. His orchestration was brilliantly colourful, his harmonies varied and rich, his rhythmic patterns constantly supple, and his solos and choruses cleverly contrasted. Though in all his operas the plots lag and the verse limps, they are nevertheless a rewarding experience for a listener who is simply interested in music.

The opera-ballet *Les Indes galantes* contains some of his freshest music. For beauty of line, nothing can be more satisfying than Huascar's airs, 'Clair flambeau du monde' and 'Permettez, astre du jour'; the way in which the melody of this last air is anticipated in the *Loure en Rondeau* that precedes it is delightful; the answering back of the chorus in 'Clair flambeau' is also masterfully contrived. He knew how to write for chorus, even though he rarely used the contrapuntal methods of Handel or Bach.

What Rameau knew better than any other composer of his period was how to contrast a series of dance measures so that every new dance sounds fresh and vital.

Historians of orchestration have often considered that Gluck was the first who consistently used orchestral instruments to obtain special effects of tone-colour. This attribution overlooks Rameau's exceptionally successful experiments earlier in the same century. As an example of entrancing colour in orchestration may be cited the *First Air for Zephyr* in the section of *Les Indes galantes* called *Les Fleurs*; or the orchestration of 'Musettes, résonnez,' with the use of the bagpipe, two piccolos, oboe, bassoons, harpsichord and strings, all interwoven with consummate skill. In the same opera-ballet Huascar's self-immolation scene provides an example of what Rameau could do towards stirring up an orchestral typhoon. The use of the orchestra for massive tonal effects is also well illustrated in the passage sung by Zima, a North American Indian maiden, as she addresses her lover Adario in the last scene.

The orchestral music used in the last episode of *Les Indes galantes* was conceived first as a harpsichord piece called *Les Sauvages*; written in 1725, ten years before *Les Indes* was produced, it was played at a Paris exhibition where captured Indians were on display. As the composition for harpsichord is complete in itself, when orchestrated it can stand alone without the singing of Zima, Adario, or chorus. But the addition of an outer vocal garment creates a fascinating tonal effect. Haydn in the first solo of his oratorio *The Seasons* tried the same effect of adding a vocal solo to instrumental music already conceived (he took the second movement of his so-called *Surprise Symphony* and added an independent voice part above it). But Rameau's experiment in *Les Sauvages* is much more elaborate and fully worked out.

The first German opera — like the first English, Spanish and Mexican — has been lost. Only the libretto which Heinrich Schütz (1585–1672) used survives. This opera, produced at Torgau during the wedding festivities of a German princely couple, was entitled *Dafne*, and the text was modelled upon that which Rinuccini had written for the lost 'first opera' at Florence. Schütz, who was trained under Giovanni Gabrieli in Venice, thoroughly assimilated the Italian style, and it is probable that had his opera survived it would have shown no pronounced departures from Italian models. Only a handful of seventeenth-century German operas remain, and they are not impressive musically. Hamburg was the most important centre of German opera at the close of this period, but even its importance was short-lived. The opera house closed in 1738, and for almost fifty years nothing but Italian opera was heard in Germany.

In order to finance the importation of Italian opera companies the petty princelings in Germany resorted to the grossest kind of exploitation. The Duke of Brunswick, for example, is reported to have sold his subjects into slavery to raise money to pay an Italian operatic troupe. Opera in Germany as elsewhere during the baroque epoch epitomized all the social abuses of the old political order. The smaller monarchs interested themselves almost exclusively in performers rather than in composers, and in performers moreover who were always Italians. Consequently German composers, even where they managed to get a hearing, as in Hamburg, were obliged for cater for Italian singers by writing Italian rather than German texts.

In England the Italian opera troupes did not gain a complete stranglehold until the early part of the eighteenth century. During the seventeenth century the Puritan conscience had reacted against spoken drama. The first English opera, produced under the Commonwealth, was disguised under the label: 'Moral Representation in Recitative Musick.' The individual acts were not called Acts, but rather Entries, in order further to disguise the dramatic element. The words of *The Siege of Rhodes*, 'the first English opera,' were written by Sir William D'Avenant, and the music by five composers, each taking one Entry (Act) as his responsibility. About the music we can say nothing, except by inference from the text; each Entry concludes with a chorus of men or of women.

During the Restoration period any play with a large amount of incidental music was called an 'opera'.

Dryden, for instance, called his *King Arthur*, for which Purcell wrote the music, a 'Dramatick Opera', though it actually included much spoken dialogue. The classification of such a work becomes difficult, especially as the total amount of music composed for it by Purcell runs in modern printed score to 169 pages, more music than appears in the printed score of a true opera like Handel's *Rinaldo* which has only 115 pages. If we wish to classify as operas all pieces so called by their authors in the seventeenth century, then we find their number large indeed. But if we restrict the count to those productions in which no spoken dialogue was allowed, the number is drastically reduced.

The most famous of English seventeenth-century operas sung throughout is Purcell's *Dido and Aeneas*. Purcell, who died in 1695 at the age of thirty-six or thirty-seven, proved extraordinarily prolific during his short life. His total output, as published by the Purcell Society, occupies more than twenty-five volumes in folio. The son of a court musician, he was brought up as a singer in the Chapel Royal and there met John Blow, a composer of some distinction, who gave him instruction. He became organist in Westminster Abbey and was appointed custodian of certain musical instruments in the king's possession. Throughout his short career he constantly composed music for weddings and birthdays in the royal family.

His *Dido and Aeneas* was written for performance by a group of schoolgirls. The first performance took place at Mr. Josias Priest's Boarding School for Young Gentlewomen in Chelsea. The date is believed to be 1689, when Purcell was about thirty. There are three acts. In the first the Carthaginian queen discourses on her love and then greets Aeneas; in the second an enchantress and a sorceress attempt to separate the pair; and in the third Aeneas departs leaving Dido heartbroken. According to Nahum Tate's libretto, each act ended with a dance, the most important being the final dance on Dido's tomb, over which Cupids scattered rosebuds.

The most famous air is Dido's Lament at the departure of Aeneas. While the bass tirelessly repeats the same pattern, Dido sings, 'When I am laid in earth.' Her melody is exactly suited to the sense of the words, and in this Lament, as in other of his melodies, Purcell showed his highest powers. Himself an excellent singer, his feeling for melody was always an exceptional asset, and indeed no one has surpassed his ability to find the right musical clothing for the English language. Particularly interesting is the way in which he managed to combine the preconceived and therefore fixed pattern in the bass, 'ground bass', with a free-flowing line in the vocal part. The reiterated bass may be likened to the powerful and inexorable chain of circumstance in which Dido finds herself entrapped,[1] while her melody can be taken to represent her desire for freedom from this bond.

Because the opera was first presented by schoolgirls a modern student might think that it would incline towards the mawkish and sentimental. But many of the principal dramas of Elizabeth's time, such as John Lyly's plays, had been performed by children, and the custom of entrusting to immature actors lines that perhaps only an adult can fully understand continued during the Restoration. A case in

---

[1] It must, however, be acknowledged that Purcell used ground bass with vastly more emotional connotations than this simile suggests, since it was his favourite unifying device.

point is an 'opera' by John Blow, Purcell's mentor. Written a few years before *Dido and Aeneas*, it was also intended for young performers. *Venus and Adonis* (as it was entitled) treated a theme which seems quite adult in its implications; but the part of Cupid was played by a tiny child, whose understanding would indeed have been precocious if she had understood all she was required to do in the action. Blow's work was termed a 'masque', but since the lines were all sung and there was music throughout, we may call it as much an opera as *King Arthur*.

Purcell provided music for two 'operas' founded on tales from Shakespeare: *The Fairy Queen* (adapted from *A Midsummer Night's Dream*) and *The Tempest, or The Enchanted Island*. As might be expected, the librettists in each case drastically altered Shakespeare, but much of Purcell's music retains a surprising interest and freshness, even after the lapse of over two and a half centuries. *The Fairy Queen* has been revived at least five times in our own century, once with a French and once with a German text. (The most notable revival took place in London, where it was successfully given with the co-operation of the Sadler's Wells Ballet.)

None of these revivals, however, can have equalled the spectacular magnificence of the first performance in 1692. The sensational scenic effects were thus described:

The Scene changes to a garden of Fountains. A Sonata plays while the sun rises; it appears red through the mist. As it ascends it dissipates the vapours and is seen in its full lustre. Then the scene is perfectly discovered, the Fountains enriched with gilding and adorned with Statues. The view is terminated by a Walk of Cypress

Trees which lead to a delightful Bower. Before the Trees stand rows of Marble Columns. Near the Top vast Quantities of Water break out of the Scene to feed the Fountains which are on each side. In the middle of the stage is a very large Fountain, where the water rises about twelve feet.

Wagner in the nineteenth century tried to revive spectacular illusions such as flying horses, transformation scenes, circles of fire suddenly springing up as if by magic; but even his most spectacular devices scarcely equalled the elaborate scenic effects of the baroque stage.

In 1691, four years before his untimely death, Purcell summed up the musical situation in England:

Musick [he wrote] is yet but in its Nonage, a forward Child, which gives hope of what it may be hereafter in *England*, when the Masters of it shall find more Encouragement. 'Tis now learning Italian, which is its best Master, and studying a little of the *French* Air to give it somewhat more of Gayety and Fashion.

Though Purcell thus foresaw the eventual dominance of Italian opera style, not until after his death did the full-scale invasion of England by Italian singers and opera composers begin. In his lifetime 'opera' could still be sung in English, but twenty years after his death only opera in Italian was sung in England.

By a strange paradox the greatest master of Italian opera was a German, who after making his name in Italy came to live in England and make his fortune here. George Frederick Handel (1685–1759), known to countless thousands today as the composer of *Messiah*, wrote this oratorio when he was fifty-six, after a life spent in composing Italian operas. He started writing these at nineteen, and his last Italian opera was completed the year before he wrote *Messiah*. Forty-six operas have been printed in the great Handel Gesellschaft (collected edition of his works).

Perhaps no opera composer in history has written more first-class music than Handel; yet his operas are no longer suitable for commercial production for the following reasons: (1) the principal male roles call for *castrati* singers; (2) the plots are poorly contrived, and the poetry with a few exceptions is inferior; (3) the operas are rigidly sectionalized.

The vocal difficulties in all the parts, not only in the *castrati* roles, are enormous. The production of an opera like *Alessandro*, which Handel specifically composed for the celebrated voices of two women, Faustina Bordoni and Francesca Cuzzoni, is an impossibility today because only once in a century can two women be brought together with such an equally fabulous voice range and quality of production. The *castrati* roles have, of course, no equivalent in our day. Farinelli, a famous *castrato* of the period, was perhaps the most remarkable singer who has ever lived. During his English engagement he received tremendous sums; and after leaving England he went to Spain where, singing the same four songs every night for the demented Philip V, he obtained such power that he was even able to dictate state policy. Senesino, a *castrato* whom Handel frequently employed, received the salary and the adulation which in our own day are reserved for Hollywood celebrities. Fourteen of Handel's operas contained parts written for Senesino.

It is impossible to rewrite operas that were tailor-made for such singers as Senesino. But even if it were possible, the absurdities of the plots would militate against their success. These plots were all based on mythology, on the lives of Greek and Roman heroes, or on medieval legend. Only in three cases, *Siroe, Poro*, and *Ezio*, did Handel use passable librettos.[1]

The one excerpt from a Handel opera still commonly heard today is the so-called 'Largo from *Xerxes*'. In this (the opening vocal solo in *Serse*), King Xerxes, singing in Italian, gives thanks for the welcome shade of a plane tree. The words of a typical Handel aria repeat themselves endlessly. Often, moreover, as in *Ombra mai fù*, they seem to us incredibly inane. Handel hardly ever used a chorus in his operas, as he did in his oratorios. In his operas he did, however, intersperse passages for all the soloists combined and almost invariably concluded his final acts with the entire cast singing together.

Two types of solo song were used: aria and recitative. Recitative, as the name implies, was a recitation (at the speed of ordinary speech). In the recitatives the singer narrated the story and kept the plot moving. The accompaniment consisted of a series of dry chords punctuating the declamation of the singer; usually these were played simply by the harpsichordist, who would have been Handel himself.

In the arias the singers do not so much narrate events as describe their reactions to them. Each aria provides the vehicle for one emotion; there is no attempt at a change of mood. In nineteenth-century opera we find the singer

---

[1] Each of these three librettos was written by the celebrated dramatic poet, Metastasio (1698–1782).

expressing anger one moment, happiness the next, envy, pity, and regret, all within the course of the same aria. This is not so in Handel's operas where he employs the principle not of chiaroscuro but of mosaic. The emotions in Handel arias are thus restricted to 'one colour per aria', as it were. The musical form of his operas often followed a pattern widely used by his Neapolitan predecessors. The latter developed an aria-type in which the opening strains of music formed one well-defined section which we can call A; followed by another well-defined section not changing the general mood, but changing the key for variety's sake, which we can call B; then the first section A was repeated. Thus the plan of such an aria-type may be expressed: $A - B - A$. (As used in arias the $A - B - A$ form is often called *da capo* form.)

In Handel's operas each key seems to have been associated with a certain emotion. C major expresses a robust and vigorous mood, F major a serene one, and G major one of exhilaration. His reaction to the different keys foreshadows the attitude of Beethoven, who called B minor 'a black tonality', and of such modern composers as Scriabin and Rachmaninoff, both of whom believed that the keys have individual personalities.

Dr. Hugo Leichtentritt has analysed the typical moods which Handel associated with each key, and also his juxtaposition of keys within an opera. The consecutive order of keys within an opera usually followed such a clearly defined plan that it can hardly have been accidental. Over a long period of time, several hours, Handel moved from key to key in an orderly fashion, suggesting forethought for the architectural plan of the whole. He was more alert than, for instance, Bach, to the psychological value of contrast-

58707

ing keys in successive movements within a large three- or
four-hour work.

After his second financial crisis Handel retired in 1741
from the life of an operatic composer and impresario. But
his instinct for the dramatic stayed with him during the last
decade of his productive life, from 1741 until 1751. In 1751
blindness overtook him as he was working at his last
oratorio, *Jephtha*. With the exception of *Messiah*, all his
oratorios are essentially dramatic works; they are operas
without costumes and scenery, rather than devotional or
contemplative works.[1]

Christoph Willibald Gluck (1714–1787), the next principal figure in operatic history after Handel, bridges the
transition period from baroque to classic. If the baroque
was an epoch of the grandiose, the classic was an epoch of
the just and balanced phrase, the perfectly measured accent.
It is in his later operas—his so-called reform operas—that
one first sees Gluck self-consciously searching for the
classic ideals of simplicity and directness of expression.
Orfeo ed Euridice, first produced in Vienna in 1762, only
three years after Handel's death, already moved in a new
world. The oldest opera that still retains its place in present-
day repertory,[2] Gluck's *Orfeo* was the most revolutionary
achievement in his career, if not the greatest.

Gluck came from Bohemia to Vienna at the age of twenty-
two, and found there a patron, Prince Melzi, willing to
help finance a period of study in Milan. In Italy Gluck
accustomed himself to the reigning style in opera; his first

[1] Further on Handel, see pp. 159–171.

[2] *La Serva padrona* by Pergolesi, originally produced at Naples in 1733 as
an 'intermezzo', is still frequently performed, but not at Covent Garden or
the Opéra.

ten operas, produced successfully in Milan and in other Italian cities between 1741 and 1745, were not distinguished. He travelled to London in 1745, met Handel, and presented two of his operas there but with only moderate success. Four years before Gluck's London visit Handel had retired from opera, but Gluck heard one or two of his oratorios. Handel also heard Gluck, but was not impressed with his technical skill as a composer, and remarked that 'he knows no more of counterpoint than Waltz, my cook.'[1] This very absence of counterpoint, however, was to become a typical feature of the new classic style. The classic spirit of the second half of the eighteenth century eschewed all attempts at interweaving separate independent melodies, and instead concentrated upon one melody at a time.

Gluck married a wealthy wife in 1750, and thus freed himself from financial worries. He was appointed a court composer at Vienna in 1755, but spent another seven years before making his final break with the conventional mannerisms of contemporary Italian opera. When the break did come and he branched out on his own he began advocating changes in the mutual relations of composer, librettist and performer, which struck his contemporaries as preposterous. Beginning with the Vienna *Orfeo ed Euridice*, he proclaimed himself in search of a new style which would embody the ideals of the antique classical spirit: 'noble simplicity and calm greatness.'

Much of Gluck's success in this particular opera must be attributed to the skill of his librettist, Ranieri Calzabigi. The wretched quality of both Handel's and Rameau's librettos has been noted. Gluck was not so unfortunate. Calzabigi was a literary craftsman of superior worth. Of

[1] Gustavus Waltz was, however, a renowned singer and no mere cook.

him Gluck wrote: 'If my music has had some success, I think it my duty to recognize that I am beholden for it to him.' He wrote significantly:

> However much talent a composer may have, he will never produce any but mediocre music, if the poet does not awaken in him that enthusiasm without which the productions of all arts are but feeble and drooping.

The libretto for *Orfeo ed Euridice* simplifies the action and is therefore easy to summarize. Before the opera opens, Eurydice has died. Orpheus in Act I is overwhelmed with grief. Amor, the God of Love, pities him and instructs him to seek her in the underworld. In Act II Orpheus descends to search for her. His entrance into the nether world is at first barred by Furies guarding the entrance to the land of departed spirits. The power of his music overcomes them, and he passes unscathed through their circle, finding his way eventually to the place of eternal happiness, the Elysian Fields. The most famous scene in the opera occurs in the Elysian Fields during the 'Dance of the Happy Spirits'. (The flute melody heard at the beginning of this scene has often been admired as one of the three or four most perfect in existence.)

In the next Act we see Orpheus leading Eurydice out of the underworld. She begs him to look at her, and is heartbroken because he will not; but Orpheus has promised not to look back. Overcome by her entreaties, however, he does look back, and at that moment she dies a second death. His overpowering sense of loss combined with the knowledge that he is responsible for this second death, is expressed in the aria 'What shall I do without my Eurydice? Whither shall I go without my beloved?' But by another intervention Amor restores Eurydice a second time, and the opera ends happily.

The music throughout is chaste and statuesque. Although the part of Orpheus in the first production was sung by a *castrato*, the vocal part was pruned and the frills cut out.

The next collaborative venture of Gluck and Calzabigi was *Alceste*, again a Greek subject. In his Preface to this opera Gluck signed his declaration of independence—independence of the abused mannerisms of conventional opera.

> When I undertook to set this poem, it was my design to divest the music entirely of all those abuses with which the vanity of singers, or the too great complacency of composers, has so long disfigured the Italian opera, and rendered the most beautiful and magnificent of all public exhibitions, the most tiresome and ridiculous.

After cataloguing the abuses, such as outrageous cadenzas, meaningless trills, long-held notes, inconsequential orchestral padding and arias endlessly repeated *da capo*, Gluck concluded:

> And lastly, it was my opinion, that my first and chief care, as a dramatic composer, was to aim at a noble simplicity; and I have accordingly shunned all parade of unnatural difficulty, in favour of clearness . . . and there is no rule of composition which I have not thought it my duty to sacrifice, in order to favour passion and produce effects.

The final period of Gluck's life began with the first performance of *Iphigénie en Aulide* in Paris on April 19, 1774. Marie Antoinette had been Gluck's singing pupil at Vienna, and she sponsored him in Paris. In *Iphigénie en Aulide* he created a masterpiece; its overture remains one of the best orchestral pieces composed in the eighteenth century. The plot like that of all Gluck's principal operas is based on a Greek legend, the story of Iphigenia, daughter of Agamemnon, the Greek chieftain, who sacrifices her in order to procure favourable winds to carry his ships towards Troy. Gluck's last principal opera was *Iphigénie en Tauride*, produced in Paris in 1779. In this powerful essay in the subterranean world of human emotion Gluck surpassed even himself; nothing his Italian rival, Piccinni, could do with the same subject was sufficient to save him from defeat, and Gluck was therefore able to retire to Vienna at the end of 1779 with a record of decisive victories against the 'Italian party' in Paris who had fought him furiously because of his challenge to operatic conventions.

Gluck's musical achievements may be briefly summarized: (1) he emphasized the importance of text, cutting out all useless roulades, meanderings, divagations in the vocal line; (2) he lifted the chorus to a new high point in operatic history; (3) he used the orchestra in a much more refined way than had previously been done.

His scores were not in shorthand like those of his predecessors; everything he wanted played he wrote down. He banished the ubiquitous harpsichord, which had been used like gummed tape to bind together the loose ends of eighteenth-century opera. Hector Berlioz, the greatest nineteenth-century authority on orchestration, particularly admired Gluck, and in his *Treatise on Instrumentation* (1844) quoted numerous examples from him. In Berlioz's opinion Gluck understood the colour of each individual instrument better than any composer before him.

Because Gluck's operas are more tightly knit than

Handel's, the 'excerpting' of individual solo arias is less easy. 'It seldom happens that a single air of his operas can be taken out of its niche, and sung singly, with much effect; the whole is a chain, of which a detached single link is but of small importance.' So observed Charles Burney, the English musical historian, in 1789.

Gluck is one of the two great German composers, the other being Wagner, whose achievements in opera have been the sole basis of their reputation. Wagner called Gluck his greatest predecessor in opera.

Supplementary Readings

For a résumé of early opera history, D. J. Grout's *A Short History of Opera*, Chapters I–XVI, is recommended. For individual composers the following books are suggested: Leo Schrade's *Monteverdi*; Hans Redlich's *Monteverdi*; Henri Prunières's *Monteverdi*; the same author's *Lully*; J. A. Westrup's *Purcell*; Hugo Leichtentritt's *Händel*; and Alfred Einstein's *Gluck*. Romain Rolland's *Essays on Music* contain valuable sections on Lully, Metastasio, Gluck, and Handel.

CHAPTER VI

THE GROWTH OF INSTRUMENTAL
VIRTUOSITY

The earliest surviving keyboard music in the British Isles dates from the first part of the fourteenth century. Later medieval instrumental music consisted for the most part of dances or of arrangements of liturgical selections. The instrumental music of the late Middle Ages and of the early Renaissance, because of the limitations of the instruments upon which it was performed, could not reach the high levels attained by vocal music during those periods. As bequeathed to us, much of this music is no more than a skeleton, to which players added flesh and blood by improvising around the bare written notes.

Medieval organs were sometimes huge, but their tone must usually have been coarse and their powers of expression limited. During the fourteenth and fifteenth centuries, however, the art of organ-building made important strides, especially in Germany, where organ music flourished conspicuously not only during the fifteenth and early sixteenth centuries, but also throughout the ensuing baroque era. In 1452 an important collection containing twenty-four pieces, *Fundamentum organisandi*, by the blind organist of Nuremberg, Conrad Paumann, was gathered; another blind organist, Arnolt Schlick, sixty years later in 1512 published a second important collection of fourteen pieces.

Most of Schlick's pieces like those of Paumann were arrangements of already existing Latin Church music; both composers therefore scarcely deserve to be called 'original', even though they did show skill in adapting vocal music for the organ. Throughout the sixteenth century arrangements of vocal music poured out like water; Germany was the special home of organ arrangements, but Italy and France also contributed. In Italy Bartolomeo Tromboncino in his book of *frottola* arrangements (1517) and in France a group of anonymous arrangers in a publication entitled 13 *Motetz* (printed by Pierre Attaignant in 1531) showed how already existing vocal music could be effectively reproduced on instruments such as the organ or 'espinette' (spinet).

If, however, we look for a collection of early instrumental music showing more 'originality', we can best find it in Spain, written for an instrument known as the *vihuela de mano*. The 'Music Book for Vihuela de Mano' of Luis Milán, published at Valencia in 1536, and entitled *El Maestro*, contained instrumental music unrelated to previously existing vocal models. An important group of pieces of *El Maestro* are entitled 'fantasias'; 'fantasia' meant here a fanciful piece in which the composer could give free rein to his imagination. The *vihuela de mano* resembled a modern guitar in shape. There were six strings, five of which were double strings and the sixth (the top one) a single string. If, as frequently happened, the lowest string was tuned to the bottom G on the bass clef, and the highest string to the G above middle C, then the tuning read thus from the bottom up: $G - c - f - a - d^1 - g^1$. The strings were plucked with the fingers of the right hand.

Milán himself was a sophisticated gentleman who refused to spend his time merely making tame reductions of religious pieces. His entire book was therefore devoted to secular music, and although he makes it plain in his introduction that he believes in the virtues of *canto llano* [Gregorian music] he does not fetter himself with any attempt to reproduce plainsong or polyphony based on it. In freeing himself from the bondage of Gregorian and polyphonic arrangements, he showed himself an important innovator.

He seems to have been the first composer who told the player in any systematic way how fast or how slowly to play his music. He was also the first composer who recommended the use of *rubato*, that is to say, fluctuations in tempo. There are several pieces in the book called *tentos* (or *tientos*), a term which may be translated 'studies'. Tento IV provides a good example of Milán's insistence upon tempo contrasts, the running passages to be played fast and the chords slowly. Romance III at the end of the book calls for the same contrast in tempo between passages and chords. The effect of both of these selections would, if Milán's directions were followed exactly, be extremely rhapsodic and dramatic.

Among the most immediately likeable pieces in *El Maestro* are those called *Pavanas*. The pavane has often been thought of as a stately, slow dance, but Milán indicated that his pavanes were to be played fast; we cannot be mistaken in this fast speed, because in *El Maestro* each item, as has already been said, is preceded by a tempo indication. The first four pavanes are written in the Dorian, Phrygian, Lydian, and Mixolydian modes respectively. The fifth pavane is, according to Milán, in the Hypomixolydian. In the commentary he wrote to accompany his music, he defined what he meant by modes and said his modal pieces had been written partly to help the performer understand what the musical characteristics of each mode are.

The pieces in *El Maestro* are all written in what is called *tablature*. In a tablature, each horizontal line stands for a string. In Milán's tablatures six horizontal lines are used, the top line corresponding to the top string, the second down to the second highest string, and so on. The numeral 0 means pluck the 'open' string; the numerals 1, 2, 3, 4, . . . mean pluck the string with the right hand while the left presses the string down at frets 1, 2, 3 or 4. (The modern notation used for the ukulele accompaniments in popular songs is a tablature, though not exactly the same kind that Milán used.)

One reason why the pavanes in Milán's book make perhaps a more immediate appeal than some of his other pieces is because he casts them in what we now know as four-bar phrases. In pieces where the phrases are all of equal length, the ear undoubtedly picks up the phrase patterns much more quickly than if they are unequal. Modern writers of popular music know this, and concentrate on producing music that can be divided equally throughout into four-bar phrases. Milán used this same regularity of pattern; the first pavane reads, eight bars (four plus four), eight bars, eight bars, then ten bars, then eight bars again, eight bars, and eight bars (the last chord counting for two bars). Pavane III has four groups of eight bars (totalling 32 bars) at its beginning; Pavane VI consists of three groups of eight (totalling 24).

Only a real virtuoso could tackle the pieces in the second half of *El Maestro*, if we are to believe Milán himself. The style is, of course, everywhere idiomatic to the instrument. Since notes that are plucked die away almost immediately, the ear must bind *vihuela de mano* music together in much the same way as the eye binds together pictures flashed on a cinema screen. Just as these are flashed in such rapid succession that the eye sees them as a continuous image, so with plucked notes: the ear continues to 'hear' them and to bind them even after they are no longer audible. Milán and other *vihuela* composers of the Spanish school so artfully contrived their music that it actually simulated at times the effect of sustained voices. Particularly clever was the plucking of one string in each pair of double strings for held notes, and the plucking of the other for passing notes, as prescribed by Fuenllana.

Milán's immediate successor in writing virtuoso music for the *vihuela* was Luis Narváez. Narváez was an innovator also. He wrote the first *diferencias*. A *diferencia* is what we would call a 'variation'. Contrapuntal composers before Narváez had, it is true, 'embroidered' round previously existing melodies. But they had not taken a melody or progression of chords, and repeated them several times in succession, each time adding some new kind of consistently contrived ornamentation. The *diferencias* of Narváez were pioneer works because they were successions of variations in the fuller sense of the term.

In addition to vihuelists an important Spanish organ virtuoso of the same period attained international distinction: Antonio de Cabezón (1510–1566). Cabezón was 'the first organist of his time, whose fame fills the world,' according to a contemporary description. Like other famous organists such as the fourteenth-century Francesco Landini of Florence, the fifteenth-century Conrad Paumann of Nuremberg, and Paumann's artistic successor, Schlick, Cabezón was blind. Philip II of Spain was his patron, and took Cabezón with him during several noteworthy trips to Italy, the Low Countries, and England. Philip II

married Mary Tudor, Henry VIII's elder daughter, and
Cabezón spent several months in England during 1555.
There he almost certainly met the leading musicians of the
English Chapel Royal, to whom he played his *diferencias*.
Much of the late sixteenth-century keyboard music com-
posed in England is cast in the same variation-form that
we first encounter in Spanish music.

Cabezón's compositions included not only nine sets of
diferencias, but also a large number of short liturgical pieces.
In 1557 some of his music appeared in a heterogeneous collection of keyboard pieces published at Alcalá de Henares,
but the most important surviving compositions appeared
twelve years after his death in a collection issued by his son
in 1578.

Cabezón's organ was not the immense instrument
which we know as the pipe organ today. Our pipe organs
are as large as we can afford to make them, with at least
two keyboards for the organist to play with his hands and
a pedal board of 32 notes for the feet.[1] Cabezón's organs
— at any rate, those which were carried about — had no
pedal boards; the tone differed, moreover, from that of the
modern pipe organ. But if we take into account the limitations of his instrument, we cannot fail to admire the
grandeur of his musical style.

Because like Milán's music Cabezón's was written in
tablature, though of a different kind, it long remained un-
deciphered. Cabezón's tablature, that is to say his musical
shorthand, was written on four lines instead of Milán's six.
Both used horizontal lines drawn across the page; both used
numerals written in such a way that the lines of the tabla-

[1] Pedals were first added to French organs as early as 1300. Spanish
cathedral organs had them *ca.* 1500.

ture cut through them. But the lines and the numerals, alike as they may look, signified in each instance something entirely different. Milán's horizontal lines stood for strings, with the highest line representing the top string, and so on. His numerals told the player where to press with a finger of the left hand so that the pitch of the string in question would be raised by the desired number of semitones.

Cabezón's horizontal lines stood for the four different 'voice-parts' in his harmony. He used the numerals 1 to 7 for the notes of the scale. One stood for F, 2 for G, 3 for A, and so on up the scale. He indicated higher or lower octaves by using a system of tiny dots or dashes placed to the right of his numerals. Like Milán, he used barlines to mark off equal divisions of time.

While Cabezón was in England he probably played for Thomas Tallis, a principal musician in the Chapel Royal; Tallis, who was some five years older than Cabezón, had composed much first-rate choral music long before 1555. His virtuoso keyboard music, however, all seems to have been written after that date; his two longest pieces, both with the same title, *Felix namque*, were written in 1562 and 1564. Although a surviving body of organ music written between 1525 and 1545 shows that England possessed a school of instrumental composers in early Tudor times, the real flowering of English keyboard music came at the end of the sixteenth century. Tallis, who was Byrd's teacher, showed, moreover, in both the 1562 and 1564 settings of *Felix namque* a virtuoso technique wholly unlike the music in such early Tudor collections as the *Mulliner Book*. His 1562 and 1564 keyboard music abounds in rapid runs, reiterated chords and brilliant scales, which only well-drilled fingers can play. Since Tallis's is the earliest that can be definitely termed English virtuoso music, and since he had ample opportunity to learn from the Spanish visitors during Mary Tudor's reign, a connection between the earlier virtuosos of Spain and later ones of England can plausibly be established.

The most important collection of early English keyboard music after the *Mulliner Book* is contained in the *Fitzwilliam Virginal Book*, so named because the collection belonged during the eighteenth century to Lord Fitzwilliam. It consists of 297 pieces, many of them in modern printed form occupying several pages. The most common type of music in the book is the 'theme with variations'. About twenty-five English composers are represented, as well as such important foreigners as Lassus, Caccini, and Marenzio. Most of the compositions by foreigners are keyboard transcriptions from their vocal works made by English composers of the late sixteenth century. One important foreigner, J. P. Sweelinck (1562–1621), the greatest Netherlander of the time, is, however, not represented in transcription but in four original keyboard works.

The virginal (or virginals) was the most popular Elizabethan keyboard instrument. The term 'virginal' has often been thought to have a connection with the Virgin Queen, Elizabeth, who is known to have played on this instrument, but the derivation is probably from *virga*, a Latin word meaning a rod or jack. The first printed collection of music for the instrument, containing selections by the three great virtuosos William Byrd (born 1543), John Bull (born 1563), and Orlando Gibbons (born 1583), was entitled: *Parthenia or The Maydenhead of the first musicke that euer was printed for the Virginalls*, and was published in 1611. It is certain, however, that the instrument was known not only long before 1611, but also long before Queen Elizabeth's time. The term 'virginals' had wide connotations, and was applied as early as Henry VIII's reign to several types of keyboard instrument, all producing their sounds by plucking.

In the modern piano, which did not come into being until more than a century after the English virginalists, the sounds are produced by hammers striking the strings. The result is a much more sustained tone than was possible with plucking. Virginal music, because plucking can never produce as loud a sound as striking with a hammer blow, seems more intimate than modern concert music for piano. But the pieces in the *Fitzwilliam Book* and in *Parthenia* demand extraordinary finger agility. Burney said it would take a first-class pianist at least a month's hard practice to play any of the pieces in the Fitzwilliam collection (which he knew in manuscript). Byrd, Bull and Gibbons all possessed magnificent techniques, if we may judge their abilities from the music they composed.

Byrd is represented by fifty-one items in the Fitzwilliam collection. The items in this collection are not arranged in any kind of logical order, but Byrd's virginal pieces fall conveniently under four headings: (1) dances such as pavanes and galliards; (2) arrangements of anonymous popular songs of the day (usually in the form of a tune followed by variations); (3) arrangements of music by other named composers; (4) free compositions, such as fantasias, not following any preconceived plan.

Although Byrd's liturgical music for voices shows him to be a skilled contrapuntist, his keyboard pieces are remarkably free from any learned pretensions. His only pavane exhibiting any considerable contrapuntal skill is No. 275 in the Fitzwilliam collection. This particular pavane, however, despite its ingenious canon, is set forth so nonchalantly that only the forewarned listener is likely to appreciate the learning involved. Byrd must have amazed his contemporaries with his Janus-like disposition: solemn and profound in his Latin motets, he was completely carefree and blithe in his virginal pieces. A contemporary copyist who was given the task of transcribing his keyboard pieces wrote admiringly at the end of one of the galliards: *Mr. W. Birde. Homo memorabilis.*

A Byrd arrangement of an anonymous popular song which deserves attention is his series of variations on 'O Mistris Myne'. Some have thought he chose as a theme for his half-dozen variations the song sung by Shakespeare's Feste in Act II, Scene III, of *Twelfth Night*:

> *O mistress mine, where are you roaming?*
> *O, stay and hear; your true love's coming,*
> *That can sing both high and low:*
> *Trip no further, pretty sweeting;*
> *Journeys end in lovers meeting,*
> *Every wise man's son doth know.*

Whether Shakespeare's clown who sang this song actually used the same tune cannot now be determined; as Shakespeare was foremost in drama at the time when Byrd was foremost in music it would, however, be pleasant for us to find some such connection. Another popular song which Byrd used for a series of variations is entitled 'Callino Casturame', a title corrupted from the Irish phrase meaning, 'Young lady, you are my treasure.' This interesting set

(Fitzwilliam Collection, No. 158) may be thus briefly outlined: (1) tune, written in what we would call eight bars of $\frac{6}{4}$, with cadences dividing the music into symmetrical patterns; (2) first variation, consisting of the original tune with a few added passing notes; (3) second variation, with more extensive use of running figures, alternating between the left and right hands; (4) tune in right hand, with passing notes reduced to a minimum, and with sharp rhythmical figuration assigned to the left; (5) continuous running motion divided between the hands; (6) return to less animated motion, with occasional use of displaced accent. At the very end there is a short bit of added music to give greater definition to the final cadence. In this series as in others of Byrd's variations he adhered rather exactly to the same harmonic scheme throughout the entire set. 'Callino Casturame' was certainly known to Shakespeare, since he mentioned it by name in *Henry V* (IV, iv, 4).

Other composers such as Giles Farnaby, Orlando Gibbons, Thomas Morley, and the prodigious John Bull left a body of virginal music which decisively proves that keyboard virtuosity was valued for its own sake in Tudor England. The Spanish fathered the variation form; slightly more than three-quarters of the 620 English virginal pieces which survive today were written in the form of variations on a theme. But if the Spanish fathered it, the English transfigured it into a vehicle for finger display.

The English lute-players seem also to have been outstanding virtuosos. John Dowland, one of the most famous, had an international reputation, and spent a considerable time in the service of the King of Denmark. A poem attributed to Shakespeare called *The Passionate Pilgrim* mentions

Dowland ... whose heavenly touch
Upon the lute doth ravish human sense.

The lute was a pluck-string instrument, differing in shape from Milán's *vihuela de mano*. In appearance the *vihuela de mano* resembled the guitar as we know it today; it was shaped like a figure 8 and had a flat back. But the lute, which was the most popular string instrument at this time outside Spain, had an oval contour and a curved back, and resembled a half pear with a long stalk.

The greatest organ virtuoso of the early seventeenth century, Girolamo Frescobaldi (1583–1643), was so spectacular a performer that it is said that thirty thousand people streamed into St. Peter's, Rome, to hear his first concert there. Frescobaldi's introduction to his *Toccatas* for organ gave these rules for the interpretation of his music:

1. First, this kind of performance must not be subject to strict time. . . . The music must be now languid, or now lively, in accordance with the emotional meaning of the passage.
2. In the Toccatas I have attempted . . . to plan the various sections so they can be played independently of one another. The player can therefore stop wherever he pleases, and does not have to perform all the sections.
3. The opening parts of the Toccatas should be played very slowly and with the chords broken. . . . The harmonies should be broken with both hands so that the instrument may not sound hollow.
4. On the last note of a rapid scale passage there should be a pause . . . in order to eliminate confusion of the different phrases.

5. The cadences, though written as rapid, must be performed quite sustained; as the performer approaches the end of the passage leading into a cadence, he must retard the tempo gradually.

6. If there is a trill [rapid alternation of two adjacent notes on the keyboard] in the right hand, and a passage of some kind in the left, the notes of the trill must not be divided mathematically, but the passage should be played quite freely.

7. In a rapid passage of semiquavers, every other note may be lengthened while the intervening notes are shortened.

8. Playing semiquavers in both hands at once, pause just before starting the passage in which these rapid notes occur, so that in playing the passage the agility of the hand will be more apparent.

9. When one finds the melody ornamented with a great many embellishments, it is advisable to play the passage very slowly. The speed in other numbers is left to the good taste and fine judgment of the performer.

These rules of interpretation, set down in 1614 by perhaps the greatest Italian organ virtuoso in musical history, embody so many striking ideas that they deserve frequent re-reading. Today there are performers and conductors who insist on 'playing the music exactly as written' in order to avoid any possible distortion of the composer's original ideas. This is undoubtedly required when interpreting the works of composers since Beethoven, the majority of whom have indicated precisely how they wished to be played. But Frescobaldi's rules show that: (1) freedom was allowed the player in abridging, condensing, or rearranging the order of the music he played; (2) the performer was given latitude in varying the pulse-rate in successive measures within the composition; (3) the mode of a composition, its emotional connotations, was decisive in determining the manner of execution. Frescobaldi's ideas spread far beyond Italy. He influenced German organ-playing not only through his pupils, but also through his publications. Bach so admired his music that he copied down his *Fiori Musicali* (1635) note for note.

During the Baroque period all the most significant composers were also accomplished performers. Dietrich Buxtehude (1637–1707), whose magnificent performances inspired the young Bach to walk two hundred miles as a pilgrim to hear him play at Lübeck; Johann Pachelbel (1653–1706), a German organist of superior calibre whose influence inspired Bach to copy his music by moonlight; the Austrian J. J. Froberger (1616–1667), a pioneer in showing how to modulate effectively from one key to another; and the French François Couperin (1668–1733), a refined and delicate colourist; all these were musically versatile as composers could only be during the Baroque period. Nowadays composition and performance have become such separated functions that it is important to note this versatility on the part of the Baroque composers.

Handel and Bach, too, were renowned performers. Handel was so outstanding that no one in Italy, where he lived between 1707 and 1710, could match him on the organ, and only one person, Domenico Scarlatti, was his equal on the harpsichord; while of Bach a learned critic of the day said that only Handel could touch him as a performer on any keyboard instrument. When Louis Marchand, the greatest French organist of his time, toured Germany, he would not compete with Bach because he anticipated defeat. Concerning Bach's virtuosity, we have this testimony: 'His technique is astonishing. The dexterity with which he crosses fingers and feet is scarcely to be believed, so quick are his movements. Astonishing, too, are the wide leaps he makes with them, never striking a wrong note nor violently contorting his limbs, no matter how energetically they move.'

The most outstanding harpsichord virtuoso in the history of that instrument was Domenico Scarlatti. His father, Alessandro, admired as the leader of the Neapolitan school of composers, undoubtedly composed a large number of praiseworthy operas and oratorios, but, though his merits are incontestable, his music is not performed today nearly so frequently as his son's. The reason is that the father wrote operas which are weighted down with the dated eccentricities of the Baroque period, whereas his son wrote charming and effervescent short keyboard pieces which still sound as fresh as the day they were composed. They were so brilliantly conceived in terms of the keyboard that in their transfer from harpsichord to piano they lose little of their freshness and piquancy.

The pieces which Domenico Scarlatti called Sonatas bear also an alternative title, Exercises. They are, however, transcendental exercises demanding the highest degree of virtuosity. About 600 of them have been published; perhaps not a tenth are familiar in the concert hall today, but his popularity with the public is growing and it seems possible that he will eventually be as well known as Bach and Handel, both of whom by coincidence were born in the same year as Scarlatti.

I

In 1720 Scarlatti went to Portugal as maestro of the Royal Chapel and music teacher to the Princess Maria Barbara. When nine years later she married the heir to the Spanish Crown he accompanied her to Madrid. The first volume of his *Essercizi per gravicembalo* (thirty pieces) was published at London in 1738.

In the same sense that Handel became an English composer — he was naturalized, lived in England half a century, and imbued his music with characteristic English traits, especially during the oratorio period — so Scarlatti may be classified as Spanish. He lived in Spain almost without interruption from 1720 until his death in Madrid on July 23, 1757, at the age of seventy-two. Burney, who knew and admired his music (54 Sonatas by Scarlatti had been printed in London between 1738 and 1752) said that in it 'he imitated the melody of tunes sung by carriers, muleteers and common people'. A recent Italian musicologist has added: 'Whoever observes Scarlatti's life by means of his works, must remain impressed by the influence popular Spanish music exerted on him.'

His Sonatas are short pieces, taking from two to six minutes to perform. They are usually divided in the middle, with both halves repeated. They begin with some pungent melodic or rhythmic figure, then proceed to something fresh, though not necessarily in a new key or in another mood. The effect produced is one of cheerfulness and *bonhomie*. In the second half the composer often switches on to a new track, without, however, changing the general mood or tempo. The endings of the first and of the second half are customarily alike; the first half will end in the key of the dominant, and the second will return to the tonic. There is a notable harmonic richness in Scarlatti;

he used frequent inner pedals, he favoured strongly dissonant accented passing notes and his modulations were sudden and intensely dramatic. As for tuning, Scarlatti probably favoured the same kind of 'equal temperament' as Bach; at any rate he never hesitated to use keys with as many as six sharps or flats in the signature.

A favourite virtuoso device in Scarlatti's Sonatas is the crossing of hands at lightning speed; this may be observed in such Sonatas as Nos. 107, 122, 215.[1] His repertory of devices includes a number of other effects that are just as exacting: for instance, repeated notes (16, 133, 148, 422), thirds and sixths in rapid motion (86, 107, 119), scales that sound like the cracking of a whip or a sudden wild gust of wind (7, 14, 40, 46, 73), precipitous leaps that remind one of a mountain goat leaping from crag to crag (1, 15, 18, 128), octaves in both hands at once (25), and rapid chromatics (126). Writers who have discussed Scarlatti have always drawn attention to his fondness for sudden changes from the tonic major to the tonic minor or vice versa, and for rapid tempi; a sampling of the first 50 of his Sonatas shows that 14 of them probably sound best at slow speeds while the remaining 36 sound best at fast speeds.

Scarlatti called for five octaves, extending from the lowest G on the modern piano to the G on the fourth leger line above the treble clef (for these limits, see Sonatas 1 and 128). Thus it appears that he called for a keyboard with the same range that Mozart (1756–1791) and the young Beethoven (1770–1827) knew.[2] The only composer of his time who wrote music as difficult was Bach (1685–1750).

---

[1] Longo edition (G. Ricordi).
[2] The five octaves on Mozart's piano extended from F_1 to f^2.

In a few of his compositions, such as the *Goldberg Variations*, Bach went beyond even Scarlatti in his demand for sensational virtuosity. But Bach expected the player to have at his command a harpsichord with two manuals, that is, two keyboards, whereas Scarlatti's Sonatas all call for only one.

Scarlatti was not followed in Italy by any who approached him in keyboard virtuosity, but in Spain he was succeeded by at least one composer whose music worthily carried on the traditions he had established: Antonio Soler (1729–1783). Soler's Sonatas conform to the Scarlatti pattern, but carry even further the older master's experiments in modulation. Soler prefigures the modulatory technique of the Romanticist composers of the nineteenth century, Liszt in particular. His *Llave de modulación* (Madrid, 1762) still remains a valuable treatise on this important branch of harmonic science.

Italy produced the most famous violin virtuosos of the baroque period. Among them the names of Arcangelo Corelli (1653–1713) and Antonio Vivaldi (1678?–1741) stand out. Corelli was famed for the quality of his tone while Vivaldi was admired for his greater technical ability. Both were pioneers in the development of the *concerto grosso*; Vivaldi's influence in the early growth of the *solo concerto* was paramount.

The mastery which each of these players attained was undoubtedly in large measure the result of native talent; but the level to which they lifted violin-playing was made possible because of great craftsmen like Girolamo Amati and Antonio Stradivari. The latter, the most famous violin-maker in history, was Corelli's senior by a scant ten years.

Corelli, it is thought, used an Austrian-made violin, a Stainer, but the general principles of construction which gave Cremona violins their superiority (Cremona was the home of the Stradivari and Guarneri *luthiers*) influenced Stainer and controlled his conception of violin shape and construction.

The use of a violin was prescribed as early as 1600 in Giovanni Gabrieli's *Sonata pian' e forte* (for brass instruments and violin), but during the early part of the seventeenth century viols were more often used. The members of the viol family had a softer tone than the violin; their shape lacked something of the refinement and elegance found in the classic violin; small details such as the design of the holes for the emission of sound, or the minute inlay round the outer border of the violin ('purfling'), can be noted as examples of the greater refinement in violin-construction.

Corelli's violin-playing was characterized by (1) beauty and suavity of tone; (2) variety and suppleness in bowing; (3) ardent warmth in slow movements; (4) restricted range rarely exceeding the note D above the treble clef, but calling in lower passages for well-developed finger and bow-arm technique. He published sixty Sonatas, two dozen of them called Chamber Sonatas (*Suonate da camera*) and as many Church Sonatas. All are divided into several distinct sections, called movements, each with its own tempo. A frequent number of movements is four, with the first movement slow, second fast, third slow, and fourth fast. The Chamber differ from the Church Sonatas in incorporating dance-form movements. Both Church and Chamber Sonatas won popularity even in conservative Rome, where Corelli was the protégé of a leading Cardinal, and where his instrumental music was frequently performed in churches.

Corelli favoured a style of instrumental music in which two different planes of sound constantly contrast with each other during the course of a composition. The two levels of sound are kept distinct, even though occasionally interfused. The compositions which he wrote in this style are called *concerti grossi*. The term *concerto grosso*, strictly used, means the 'large' group of instruments; the term *concertino*, in contrast, means the 'small' group. The large and the small groups are in constant dialogue with each other, and their 'conversation' provided Corelli with endless opportunities for echo effects.

The immense popularity of Corelli's *concerti grossi* can be ascribed in large part to the polish which he insisted upon in orchestral performances (he conducted his own string orchestra, presiding from the first violin chair). Just as in his solo Sonatas for Violin, so in his *concerti grossi* refinement, elegance and polish distinguished his style. The elder Scarlatti, commenting upon his manner of performance, said: 'There is nothing particularly remarkable in his compositions, but the extremely refined manner of execution which he insists upon is most remarkable. In playing with the other strings he demands absolute uniformity in the bowing. Each player must raise and lower his arm at exactly the same instant. His music therefore gives as much delight to the eye as to the ear.'

Vivaldi, a Venetian priest who toured as a violinist, was influenced by Corelli but went beyond him. Favoured by the Pope and by the reigning Emperor of Austria, he succeeded in astounding all who heard him. He used what are called the sixth, seventh, and eighth positions freely. These positions call for the placing of the fingers much higher up on the finger-board than Corelli ever demanded. Vivaldi is credited with popularizing what is known as half-shift; he also made extensive use of passages in which an open string rapidly alternates with an adjacent stopped string (a device known as 'bariolage'). He used incredibly long groups of staccato notes under one bow, and indulged in other bowing intricacies. His insistence upon variety in dynamics was a notable feature of his style. In his writing of concertos he is credited with having been the first to place a cadenza (a solo passage exhibiting the skill of the star performer) just before the final outburst from the whole orchestra concluding a movement (the whole orchestra playing together is called a 'tutti').

Vivaldi's music has recently enjoyed a remarkable and well-merited renascence. No one influenced the young Bach more beneficially than Vivaldi, 'the Red priest' (his hair was red). Other Germans besides Bach came under his influence, but Bach's indebtedness is perhaps the most easily proved; for he transcribed nine complete concertos of Vivaldi, rearranging them for keyboard instruments (harpsichord and organ). According to J. N. Forkel, who wrote the first biography of Bach, Vivaldi was the composer's best 'teacher'. In his youth Bach had no formal instruction in composition. 'The Violin Concertos of Vivaldi, which had just been published, provided him with the necessary guide. From them he learned how to develop his ideas, how to dispose his key relations, how to vary his modulatory devices, and how to do many other necessary things.' Vivaldi's *Estro Armonico* (Harmonical Whim), a collection of concertos, was published about the year 1712. Bach lived in Weimar from 1708 until 1717, and it was towards the end of his time there that he showed a remarkable enrichment in instrumental style. Undoubtedly this was due to the influence of Vivaldi.

Vivaldi wrote some 469 concertos, most of which are now available in modern reprint. He did not confine himself to violin concertos; there are a great number for bassoon as well as less familiar instruments. He gave many of his concertos fanciful names, such as 'The Seasons'. In his use of titles he endeavoured exactly to express poetical ideas in music; in 'The Seasons', for instance, he illustrated in musical terms the ideas found in four sonnets on spring, summer, autumn and winter. Such 'programme' music is discussed with some fullness in a note on p. 147.

As Vivaldi used the term, concerto came more and more to mean the contrast between a solo performer and an orchestra, rather than between a small and a large group of performers. In his concertos we see the instinct of the virtuoso everywhere at work. As a single player he was able to develop his own part to a much more dazzling pitch than a group of players could ever hope to attain. One person alone can always, if he wishes, polish his part to the utmost; but several performers working as a team often fail to bring their parts to the perfection which they might singly achieve. Vivaldi therefore thrust aside the old idea of co-operation in the concerto form, and substituted instead the idea of *domination*.

SUPPLEMENTARY READINGS

Gilbert Chase, *The Music of Spain* (pp. 51–74, 106–117)
J. B. Trend, *Luis Milán and the Vihuelistas*

Frederick Dorian, *The History of Music in Performance* (pp. 51–87)

R. Thurston Dart, *The Interpretation of Music*

Manfred Bukofzer. *Music in the Baroque Era* (pp. 222–239)

Wilfrid Mellers, *Francois Couperin and the French Classical Tradition*

Ralph Kirkpatrick, *Domenico Scarlatti*

Marc Pincherle, *Corelli*

Marc Pincherle, *Vivaldi et la musique instrumentale*

For a comprehensive list of sources, see Thurston Dart's excellent manual, pp. 181–183, and for further secondary material p. 185.

CHAPTER VII

THE CULMINATION OF THE BAROQUE EPOCH

Bach and Handel, the foremost composers of the Baroque period, were both born in 1685. The distance separating their birthplaces was only a little over eighty miles. Both grew up in a strongly Lutheran milieu. Yet despite these similarities, the two men did not share the same musical outlook.

Bach sequestered himself in the environment from which he sprang, and during the whole of his lifetime never travelled over an area larger than about three hundred square miles. Handel, on the other hand, travelled to Italy in 1707, and returned for a second visit in 1729. He settled in England with London as his headquarters in 1710, but travelled as far afield as Dublin, where he gave the first performance of *Messiah* in 1742. Bach, though early recognized as a virtuoso, achieved no more than a local reputation as a composer, and was forgotten during the half-century after his death in 1750. Handel, on the contrary, won immediate recognition as a composer as well as a performer — in Hamburg, Rome, Venice, London and Dublin, to name only the places he personally visited. When Bach died, he was placed in a grave the site of which was soon forgotten. When Handel died he was interred in Westminster Abbey.

Bach spent the greater part of his mature years in the service of the Lutheran Church. His position as cantor of the Thomasschule at Leipzig entailed such onerous duties as teaching Latin to unwilling youths. He was expected to

produce a weekly stream of music suitable for the ceremonies of the Church; he trained his own choirs and
taught his own singers. Handel spent only one year, his
eighteenth, as a church organist, and upon quitting Halle,
his home town, permanently abandoned Church work.
Not only his operas but also his oratorios were produced
with the assistance of paid professional singers. Never did
he present such an oratorio as *Messiah* or *Israel in Egypt* in
church.

Bach wrote his sacred masterpieces, the *St. John Passion*,
the *St. Matthew Passion*, for use in Church services.
Handel's oratorios were intended as commercial entertainments during the Lenten season, when theatres were
forbidden to present operas; they were always commercial
enterprises, even though the money occasionally went to
charities. By a strange quirk Handel has come to be
regarded as a 'religious' composer, while Bach, who really
was a religious composer, in the proper sense of the word,
has been neglected in churches, to which his music right-
fully belongs.

Albert Schweitzer, perhaps the greatest twentieth-cen-
tury authority on Bach, once said that a mere knowledge of
Bach's life helped little in preparing a student for an understanding of his music. Schweitzer was right if by the facts
of Bach's life he meant a bare catalogue of dates and places
where he lived. Such a catalogue might read: at Eisenach,
his birthplace, until his father's death in 1695; at Ohrdruf
in his elder brother's charge for the next five years; at
Lüneburg as a chorister from 1700 until 1703; at Arnstadt
as an organist from 1703 until 1707; at Mühlhausen in
similar capacity for a year; at Weimar as Court Organist

and Concertmeister from 1708 until 1717; at Cöthen as
Capellmeister from 1717 until 1723; and at Leipzig as
Cantor and *Director Musices* for the remaining twenty-seven
years of his life.

But clothed in a living body of flesh and blood the
skeleton of places and dates can take on meaning and can
help us understand Bach's musical accomplishment. Johann
Sebastian Bach came of a long line of professional musicians
of that family name. This musical pedigree so impressed
J. N. Forkel, Bach's first biographer, that in a Life comprising only eleven chapters he devoted one entirely to
Bach's ancestry.

Bach, *the* Bach, since all other members of the family
are dwarfed beside him, grew up without formal advantages in education. His elder brother, Johann Christoph,
took him under his care when he was left an orphan at the
age of ten. He seems to have remained indifferent to his
musical advancement, and went so far as to remove a
volume of music which the young Sebastian had copied
painfully by moonlight in an effort to educate himself.
This nocturnal copying graphically illustrates his perseverance in carrying to completion the hardest tasks in order
to improve himself. Here is the anecdote as it appeared in
his obituary:

His brother possessed a book of clavier pieces by the
most famous masters of the day — Froberger, Kerl,
Pachelbel — and this, despite all his pleading and for
who knows what reason, was denied him. His zeal to
improve himself thereupon gave him the idea of practising the following innocent deceit. This book was kept
in a cabinet of which the doors consisted only of grill-

work. Now, with his little hands he could reach through the grillwork and roll the book up (for it had only a paper cover); accordingly, he would fetch the book out at night, when everyone had gone to bed, and since he was not even possessed of a light, copy it by moonlight. In six months' time he had these musical spoils in his own hands. Secretly and with extraordinary eagerness he was trying to put it to use, when his brother, to his great dismay, found out about it, and without mercy took away from him the copy he had made with such pains. We may gain a good idea of our little Johann Sebastian's sorrow over this loss by imagining a miser whose ship, sailing for Peru, has foundered with its cargo of a hundred thousand thalers.[1]

Particularly important in this story is the phrase, 'his zeal to improve himself.' Throughout his adolescence and early manhood one encounters numerous instances of the same zeal. Without formal education, and certainly without money, he undertook the hardest tasks and the most difficult journeys to improve himself.

On several occasions while a member of the choir at Lüneburg he travelled on foot to Hamburg, a distance of thirty miles, to hear the celebrated organist, Reinken, who was then approaching his eightieth year. An anecdote that has often been retold illustrates his perseverance. Returning after one of these walking journeys to Hamburg, he was destitute, and in his hunger picked up two herring-heads that had apparently been cast out as refuse. Inside each he found a Danish coin some kindhearted soul had inserted.

[1] Translated in *The Bach Reader* (ed. by H. T. David and A. Mendel), p. 217.

Bach gladly ate the remnants of the fish and used the Danish ducats for a return trip to Hamburg.

After moving to Arnstadt, where at only eighteen he was appointed church organist, he went again on a pilgrimage on foot, this time to Lübeck, a journey of over 200 miles. There he heard the great Dietrich Buxtehude, then in his late sixties. When he could not hear an artist in the flesh, he studied his music by transcribing it. Forkel testified to his unremitting labours as copyist and arranger; Vivaldi, in particular, was a model he repeatedly copied. 'He never neglected at the same time to study with the greatest attention the works of Frescobaldi, Froberger, Pachelbel, Buxtehude, Reinken, and some old French organists, who . . . were all great masters of harmony and of the fugue.'

Though self-educated Bach showed from the start breadth of vision; he used as his models composers of several nationalities. His music thus reflected his acquaintance with his greatest predecessors and contemporaries in Italy, France, and Germany. As late as 1714, when he was already a master, he copied Frescobaldi; still later, he made an arrangement with continuo of an *a cappella* composition by Palestrina. In 1720 and in 1729 his eager, though futile attempts to meet Handel, who in those years visited Halle, his home town, show his alertness even in maturity and his continuing desire for wider horizons. Unable to meet Handel personally, he learned from him by copying one of his Italian cantatas.

In his own music Bach was able to assimilate Italian, French, and German traits. In writing his *Concerto in the Italian Style* or his *Overture in the French Manner*, moreover, he was able to keep clearly distinct and apart from each other the traits of the different national schools. It was his ability to grasp the essence of a particular style, and then make it something peculiarly his own, that distinguished Bach from his lesser contemporaries. He never slavishly imitated; on the contrary, he so perfectly assimilated the elements of a given style that he could write in one Partita an Italian Corrente and in another a French Courante.

Bach's three principal periods were the Weimar, the Cöthen, and the Leipzig. At Weimar he wrote brilliant virtuoso pieces for organ; at Cöthen, secular music, notably the Brandenburg Concerti Grossi and other concerted music for orchestra; and at Leipzig, Church music, such as Passions and Cantatas. His last decade showed a return to secular projects on a vast scale, notably the *Goldberg Variations*, the *Musical Offering*, and the *Art of Fugue*.

He married twice, first (at twenty-two) his cousin Maria Bach; and second (at thirty-six) Anna Magdalena Wülcken, daughter of a professional musician. Anna Magdalena had a fine, clear voice, and helped him by her singing and by her music copying. She received her elementary instruction from her husband, and the notebook of pieces that he wrote for her early lessons is often used today to instruct young pianists. She survived him, and died penniless in 1760, ten years after his death.

Of Bach's seven children by his first wife, Wilhelm Friedemann, the eldest son, talented but profligate, and Carl Philipp Emanuel (1714–1788), talented and industrious, are the best known. Of his thirteen children by his second wife (many of whom died in infancy), Johann Christian (1735–1782), the youngest son, stands out most prominently. Both Carl Philipp Emanuel and Johann Christian in fact became far more famous in their own day than their father had been in his. Carl Philipp Emanuel helped to inaugurate a new style of music and effectively influenced such first-rate musicians as Haydn and Mozart. Johann Christian went to London and after Handel's death became the darling of the British public. There his operas were produced at enormous expense, and everything he wrote was immediately successful, because, unlike his father, he wrote for his own generation.

J. S. Bach deliberately chose the life of a church musician, though his own father had been a professional town musician unconcerned with church duties and without family connections that might have impelled him to choose the church. His first organ appointment at Arnstadt, which ceased when he was twenty-two, ended unhappily because he was a perfectionist. He then went to Mühlhausen, where again this obsession caused friction. He left after only a year. In his letter of resignation he told the Mühlhausen church authorities: 'I have always liked to work toward the goal of perfection in Church music, and my one objective has been the glory of God.' His difficulties at Mühlhausen were not entirely of his own making; the churches there were torn with strife. One faction wanted the barest simplicity in Church music, while others of the older party were favourably disposed toward elaboration.

In Weimar, where he lived for nine years, Bach escaped for a time from church duties. The list of Weimar organ pieces includes some of his most brilliant compositions: among them the *Toccata and Fugue in D minor*, the *Prelude and Fugue in D Major*, the *Prelude and Fugue in A minor*, and the *Toccata, Adagio, and Fugue in C Major*. His own sensational skill as an organist enabled him to create effects that have not since been surpassed. In addition to his brilliant concert pieces, Bach also wrote at Weimar a *Little Organ Book*, the full title of which reads: 'In which a Beginner at the Organ is given instruction in Developing a Chorale in many different ways, and at the same time in Acquiring Facility in the Study of the Pedal.'

The *Little Organ Book*, which Bach is thought to have written while in prison, contains the only organ pieces from this period which are distinctly sacred in nature. (He was imprisoned by Duke Ernst August of Weimar, who resented his application for release from service. Bach was a good enough servant of the Duke at other times; his only crime was his desire to take up a more remunerative appointment.) But though many of his pieces written at Weimar and most of those written during his next period at Cöthen are secular, his eventual decision to re-enter the service of the Church, even though it meant loss of prestige, indicates that a religious atmosphere was more to his nature. Otherwise he need not have left Cöthen, where his title of Capellmeister lent him some consequence, to become a Cantor at Leipzig. That his sons were placed in a small Lutheran school while he was at Cöthen (which was not a Lutheran centre), shows that Bach was extremely conscientious in the discharge of his family responsibilities, and wished his sons to grow up with what he considered a suitable religious background.

At Leipzig he gave the Town Council an understanding to do the following:

(1) Set the boys who attended the choir school a shining example of an honest, retiring manner of life.

(2) Bring the music in both the principal churches of the town into good estate, to the best of his ability.

(3) Show the Town Council all proper respect and obedience . . .

(4) Faithfully instruct the boys not only in vocal but also in instrumental music.

(5) So arrange the music that it would not last too long, and would not sound like an opera, but rather incite the listeners to devotion . . .

(6) Treat the boys in a friendly manner and with caution, but, in case they do not wish to obey, punish them with moderation or report them to the proper place.

(7) Faithfully attend to the instruction in the school . . .

(8) Not go out of town without the permission of the Honourable Burgomaster.

(9) Always walk with the boys at funerals [singing at funerals was an important duty of the choirboys].

(10) Not accept or wish to accept any office in the University without the consent of the Council.

Yet in spite of all these restrictions on his liberty Bach was free to produce his own music week after week in the Leipzig churches. He could use the choirboys in performances of his works, and had an orchestra at his disposal. He also enjoyed certain material advantages: lodging in the school buildings, for instance, not only for himself but for his family. The age of his singers told in his favour also. They were youths between the ages of ten and twenty; heavier men's voices were sometimes added. He thus had a more pliable group than has the average modern choir-director.

The principal Sunday service at Leipzig during Bach's time lasted five hours, out of which half an hour or so was taken up with one of his cantatas. Because of the rigidly set

Church calendar he had the advantage of knowing the subject of the sermon well in advance. His cantatas were musical illustrations of the Biblical text set for the sermon. Their librettos usually contained sentences of Scripture, to which was added a poetical meditation on the texts. Bach was able to employ the services of local poets to write the words for his works. One of these was a rhymester who used the pseudonym of Picander. Picander's verse rarely equals Bach's music, but at least he was willing to write to order.

In his later Leipzig years Bach's output of church music diminished. He had personal difficulties with the Rector (headmaster) of the Thomasschule. The youthful J. A. Ernesti, who became Rector in 1734, hated music and discouraged the members of the choir school from taking it up as a profession. When he came across a student practising he would disdainfully exclaim: 'What? You want to be a beer-fiddler, too?' Ernesti, moreover, had the ear of the Burgomaster, the most influential man in Leipzig. The trouble between Bach and Ernesti ostensibly arose because Bach refused to accept as a prefect a certain student named J. G. Krause. Bach was responsible for the music in four churches, but actually attended two alternately, the Thomas and Nicholas Churches. He was allowed the assistance of a prefect who (acting as deputy conductor) enabled him to perform his Sunday duties. Ernesti tried to force upon him an assistant whose musical abilities were wholly inadequate. Both parties appealed to the Town Council, the controlling authority. Ernesti accused Bach of disingenuous conduct, and even of downright dishonesty. Eventually by taking his case to the King of Saxony, who ruled Leipzig from his capital at Dresden, Bach won what amounted to a Pyrrhic victory. He secured a non-resident appointment at the Dresden court as *Composer to the Court Chapel*, in November, 1736, and thenceforth turned his mind to other matters. After his troubles with Ernesti had come to a head he no longer enjoyed cordial relations with his choristers, many of whom were intimidated. With the deterioration in personal relations, he could no longer count on any wholehearted co-operation, and stopped writing large-scale church works during the last ten years of his life.

The monumental works such as the *St. John Passion* (1723), the *Magnificat* (1723), the *St. Matthew Passion* (1729), and the *Christmas Oratorio* (1734-5), were all produced during his first twelve years at Leipzig. He composed no new large-scale church works after Ernesti became headmaster. True, he did finish the *Mass in B minor*, but this huge work was not intended for performance at Leipzig, but rather as a tribute to the reigning King of Saxony. Of the 300 cantatas which he is reputed to have written (a small percentage of these were on secular subjects) approximately 200 survive today. Of the extant church cantatas, only one can be securely dated after 1740, and the vast bulk of them seem to have been written during the first few years at Leipzig which saw the production of the great works already mentioned.

After the break with Ernesti, Bach turned his attention to secular composition. In 1739, ten years after the *St. Matthew Passion*, he was no longer interested either in writing a new Passion or in resurrecting an old one. He told the clerk of the Town Council that the production of a Passion on Good Friday was 'only a burden'. Without wholehearted co-operation from the singers and the headmaster such an undertaking could only have been a trial.

In 1742 Bach published his famous set of thirty variations for harpsichord with two manuals, now known as the *Goldberg Variations*. In 1744 he completed the second Part of *The Well-Tempered Clavier*, which like Part I contained twenty-four preludes and fugues in all the twenty-four major and minor keys.[1] In 1747 he finished another large work, *The Musical Offering*, consisting of assorted canons, *ricercars*, and a trio sonata for flute, violin, and *continuo*, all constructed on a 'royal theme' which he was given to improvise upon when he visited Frederick the Great at Potsdam during that year. At the time of his death in 1750 he was engaged in writing *The Art of Fugue*, a compendious collection of fugues, all of them growing out of the same melodic germ. When he found he could not complete *The Art of Fugue* because of blindness he stopped work on it in the middle of a fugue, and dictated his last composition, a setting of a chorale that bore these words:

Before Thy throne, my God, I stand;
Myself, my all, are in Thy hand;
Turn to me Thine approving face,
Nor from me now withhold Thy grace.

Grant that my end may worthy be,
And that I wake Thy face to see,
Thyself for evermore to know !
Amen, Amen, God grant it so !

(translated by C. S. Terry)

A survey of Bach's creative accomplishment shows that he preferred to work in the sacred forms as long as he could pursue his ideals of perfection; but since he would not

[1] 'Well-Tempered' means 'equally tuned', i.e. with all the semitones of the same size.

compromise, he occasionally encountered such resistance that he had to turn elsewhere for creative satisfaction. When he sent his *Musical Offering* to Frederick the Great he said in his dedication: 'This resolve has now been carried out as well as possible.' Everything he set his hand to, from the simplest two-part invention to the six-part *Sanctus* of the *Mass in B minor*, he carried out 'as well as possible'.

Bach's music appeals to present-day concert audiences because he combined profound emotional fervour with superb craftsmanship. He expressed sublimely such emotions as awe and wonder in the presence of Omnipotence. His music encompasses profound love, reverent trust and the deepest yearning, and he knew how to portray in musical symbols the ideas of grandeur and of unleashed power. On occasion he could also throw discretion to the winds, and slip into jocose and playful moods. His music is comparable to Milton's poetry.

Schweitzer, his biographer, has given several helpful clues to assist us in understanding Bach's message. He found in his works an exhaustive vocabulary of musical symbols. By musical symbol he meant a melodic or rhythmic idea which Bach consistently used to express the same general type of emotion. A rhythm of a dotted quaver followed by a semiquaver, used over and over again, expressed the idea of dignity or solemnity. A rhythm such as this:

expressed such emotions as 'terror, horror, and despair'. Bach used this rhythmic figure

to express 'charm and happiness', and he used the following:

to express 'joy of a naïve kind'. For each type of emotion Schweitzer thought he was able to adduce an exact musical symbol. If the symbol were not a rhythmic one, it might be a melodic one. The bass slowly descending in chromatic intervals suggested grief, despair. The bass line going down in diatonic scale steps, but with ties so that each new tone sounds on a weak part of the beat,

was used, Schweitzer thought, to express exhaustion or weakness.

Bach was able to portray with musical symbols 'some one standing on a rolling ship and planting his feet wide apart in order to keep a firm footing', or 'the drooping of the exhausted body of Jesus on the cross', or 'the strong arm of the Saviour drawing mankind upward to rescue it from Hell', or 'the restless heaving of the waves and then the bursting of the storm', or 'the motion of flowing water and the glassy surface of a lake', or 'the contortions of a serpent, and the angry stamping of the heel to crush its head'. The method Schweitzer used to find a symbol was to look at various examples of Bach's 200 cantatas, or other choral works, with his eye constantly on the text; in his opinion Bach always used the same kind of symbol to

express the same kind of emotion. Wherever two different motives are used in the same piece, either in close
succession or simultaneously, then, Schweitzer said, we
may be sure Bach is illustrating two diverse emotions
which occur in close succession or simultaneously. He
illustrated this by referring to certain cantatas where the
words express the thought of Christ's suffering (sorrow
motive) and then immediately afterwards the idea of joy
in salvation (joy motive); he continued his list of illustrations with enough specific instances of motives used in
close juxtaposition or simultaneously to establish his point.
Schweitzer's whole case rests on the study of Bach's choral
work where words were illustrated in music. Whether the
same motives that recur constantly in his vocal music also
meant the same thing in his music without words cannot
be proved, but Schweitzer believes that the motives,
whether they appeared in vocal or in instrumental music,
always conveyed a definite and recognizable meaning.

Anyone who wished to study Bach's musical language
with Schweitzer as his guide would begin by studying the
motives. He would listen to the opening chorus of Cantata
No. 78, and follow them: the first motive expressing
anguish followed by the second expressing joy.[1] Or he
would listen to the *Crucifixus* of the *B minor Mass* and feel
the poignancy of the descending motive of grief. Or he
would hear the violin solo of the *Laudamus te* from the same
Mass and notice the motive of 'joy of a naïve kind', to
which we referred:

---

[1] *Bach-Gesellschaft* XVIII, 257–268.

Or he would listen to the *Credo* of the same Mass, particularly observing the 'measured, tranquil descending scale steps that indicate resolution and confident faith.'

An example of obvious tone-painting occurs at the end of an alto solo in the *Magnificat*, where a chord expected and desired by the hearer is purposely left out. At this point the words read, 'The rich he hath sent empty away'. Bach symbolizes the emptiness by omitting a resolution the hearer confidently expects. Another striking effect in the same work is obtained by the entrance of the chorus on the words *omnes generationes*, 'all generations.' In the tenor aria *Deposuit* there is a rush of scale steps downwards on the words, '*He hath put down* the mighty from their seats,' and then the equally effective climb upwards on the words, '*And hath exalted* them of low degree.' In the chorus 'He hath showed strength,' words and music unite in a display of rhythmic power.

One of Bach's most formidable achievements is his *B minor Mass*. This lengthy work is divided into twenty-four different numbers.[1] Unlike sixteenth-century composers Bach did not divide the Mass-text into five self-contained movements but took each of the five classic divisions and subdivided them again into smaller units. In each of these smaller units he then repeated words a large number of times with the result that each number became a self-contained artistic unity. But the Mass was greatly lengthened by such textual repetitions, and Bach's lasts well over two-and-a-half hours. In his time, these repetitions in settings of the Mass-text had become customary,

---

[1] Two numbers (6 and 24), though set to different portions of the Mass-text, employ the same music. By this repetition Bach enhanced the overall unity.

especially in Italy. As he used Vivaldi frequently for a model, and learned from him, it may be instructive to compare the Gloria of the *B minor Mass* with Vivaldi's *Gloria Mass*. It will be found that Bach followed Vivaldi not only in the division of the text, but also in the assignment of certain sections to solo voices and others to chorus. Vivaldi split up the *Gloria* into eleven different numbers, Bach into eight. Vivaldi, moreover, will be found to have been even more frolicsome than Bach in certain portions of his *Gloria*, as in Nos. 8 and 9.

Unlike the *St. Matthew Passion*, which contains no fugues, the *Mass in B minor* begins and ends with choral fugues. The Passions frequently used recitative; borrowed from opera, this device enabled a singer to tell a story or give an account of events at a rapid pace. In the *Mass*, however, no recitations of the text in this style appear. Five of the twenty-four movements are written in B minor; the others, with one exception, are in closely related keys: D Major, G Major, E minor, A Major, and F sharp minor. The one exception is a movement in G minor, which because it employs two flats is not classified as a closely related key to B minor with two sharps. Though Bach uses seven different keys in the course of this vast work his contemporary, Handel, used a much greater variety in such large choral works as *Israel in Egypt* and *Messiah*.

Bach's orchestra for the *Mass in B minor* consisted of two flutes, two oboes, alternating with two oboes d'amore (an instrument akin to the present-day English horn), two bassoons, one horn (*corno da caccia*), three trumpets, kettledrums, and strings. There was also a part for a harpsichordist or organist, called the *continuo*. The written continuo part, a shorthand indication of the harmonies that were to be played, is a bass part with numerals telling what intervals must be played above the bass. The *continuo* parts were also called *basso continuo*, or figured bass. (All Bach's and Handel's orchestral music used figured bass, and only with the advent of the Viennese classicists did this 'filler' provided by harpsichord or organ drop out of the orchestral score.)

Bach's one excursion into the field of programme music[1] was his *Capriccio written on the Departure of a Favourite Brother*. (The departure of his brother Johann Jacob for Poland, where he had the promise of a position in the army

[1] By definition 'programme music' means that class of instrumental music which uses descriptive titles, and which tells a story or paints a picture. Programme music was written as early as the sixteenth century; Byrd wrote a series called, quaintly, 'Mr. Byrd's Battle' with the following titles: (1) the march before the battle; (2) the soldier's summons followed by the march of the footmen and of the horsemen; (3) the sound of the trumpets; (4) an Irish march; (5) bagpipe, drone, flute; (6) march to the fight; (7) tantara, tantara, the battle starts, followed by the retreat of the enemy; (8) galliard for victory; (9) burying of the dead; (10) morris dance; (11) soldiers' dance. A French composer named Jannequin wrote some charmingly descriptive music during the same century. Later composers in France continued the tradition of programme music, and almost contemporary with Bach were such masters of the type as Couperin and Rameau. The Cantor who preceded Bach at Leipzig, Kuhnau, was a writer of programme music. His Biblical Sonatas told stories such as David's fight with Goliath. In writing his Capriccio at the time of his brother's leaving, then, Bach was following an old tradition. The advantages of a programme piece are obvious. The listener knows what he is supposed to hear. On the other hand, he is left free to form his own images and construct his own programme, if the title is not explicit. The opposite of programme music is 'abstract' or absolute music. Generally speaking, advanced musicians prefer to listen to absolute rather than to programme music. If the latter becomes too imitative, the effect may prove inartistic. For instance, a storm can be portrayed as Liszt portrayed it in his *Orage*. But the closer the sound gets to that of an actual storm, the less interesting does it become as music. If one wants to listen to a storm, the best way is to get out in one. If one wants to listen to a nightingale, the best way is to listen to a recording of its song, not to Liszt's *Le Rossignol*.

of the Swedish King, Charles XII, as oboist.) Composed for clavier in 1704, when he was only nineteen, this Capriccio was divided into six short sections, each with a descriptive title: (1) an entreaty made by the brother's friends, who do not wish him to leave on his journey; (2) their listing of the various misfortunes that may overtake him in foreign lands; (3) a general lament by his friends; (4) their bidding him farewell, since they realize they cannot dissuade him from going; (5) the sound of the postilion; (6) fugue in imitation of the postilion horn.

The keyboard instruments used by Bach were the organ, the harpsichord, and the clavichord. In general he seems to have preferred the harpsichord for brilliant music, and the clavichord for meditative music. The harpsichord, whose notes were produced by plucking, was a less intimate instrument than the clavichord, whose notes were produced by metal tangents which did not pluck but rather pressed the string. Bach's harpsichord, unlike Scarlatti's, possessed two keyboards, one above the other. He did not write for the piano. In 1747 when he visited Frederick the Great at Potsdam, and was rushed before the eager king without being given time to change his wig and get out of his travel clothes, he did have an opportunity to test the pianos which the king owned. But the piano was not invented until about 1709[1] and was therefore in its infancy during Bach's lifetime.

It is not always possible to determine what instrument Bach had in mind, harpsichord or clavichord, in writing various pieces. The most famous collection of his keyboard music, *Das Wohltemperierte Clavier*, 'The Well-Tempered

[1] By a Florentine, Bartolommeo Cristofori (1655–1731).

Keyboard,' contains items clearly designed for harpsichord (such as the Prelude in G sharp minor, Part II) and others suitable for the clavichord (such as the E flat minor Prelude in Part I). The complete collection contains forty-eight ...eludes and Fugues, twenty-four in Part I (1722) and another twenty-four in Part II (1744). Bach was a pioneer in writing pieces in all the major and minor keys. For their performance a system of tuning was necessary which, though now universal, was then only just coming into vogue. The types of tuning used before the 'well-tempered' method restricted the player enormously. With the older method only a few keys were in tune, and any adventurousness in modulation was impossible.

Bach's *Well-Tempered Clavier* contains some of his choicest music. In form the preludes differ among themselves; but they all take some melodic or harmonic idea stated at the outset, and develop that idea to its fullest. The preludes in Part II are particularly rich and varied; often presented with repeat signs in the middle and at the end, they include some of his most easily accessible music. Beethoven is recorded to have chosen as his favourite among the forty-eight the Prelude in F minor from Part II.

Bach's fugues cannot be properly appreciated without some knowledge of their structure. The word *fugue* comes from the Latin *fuga*, flight. A short melody, heard at the beginning alone, 'flies' like a bird from branch to branch throughout the fugue, appearing first on one bough and then on another. There are normally three or four voices in a fugue. Actually, of course, 'voices' are not singing, but as the fugue was originally a type of vocal music, the terminology has been kept in all discussions of it. After the initial melody has been 'sung' at the opening of the fugue by Voice I (which may lie in the soprano, alto, tenor, or bass range), it is then 'sung' by Voice II, while Voice I continues with a second melody blending agreeably with the first (now being sung by Voice II). Then Voice III enters, and follows a similar course. The starting melody is called the 'fugue subject'. There are a large number of rules governing the types of intervals which must be used in the 'subject' and in the 'answer'. There are also important distinctions to be made between real and tonal fugues, between fugues where a countersubject is developed and those where it is not. There are procedures governing cadences to be used at the end of the 'exposition', places where 'strettos' may be used, the use of devices such as 'augmentation', 'diminution', and so on. The emotional element in Bach's fugues is often easy to seize, even for an untrained hearer, but the sense of fulfilment is greater if the hearer also takes the trouble to acquaint himself with the rules of the game. The *sine qua non* in enjoying fugues is comprehended in this simple rule: Learn the opening melody by heart and then keep listening for it. It will not disappoint the hearer, because the piece is bound to contain a great many fugue 'entries'.

It is significant that the Fugue listed as No. 8 in Part I (in E flat minor) is one of the most intricate in the entire collection. There are inversions, strettos and three augmentations — enough devices to keep the puzzle-solver happy for hours. Yet this complicated fugue is also one of the most appealing as pure music.

Bach's keyboard music includes besides the *Well-Tempered Clavier* nineteen dance suites, half-a-dozen toccatas, and a number of independent compositions such as the famous *Chromatic Fantasia and Fugue*, which 'for all its technical skill, appeals to the most unpractised hearer, if it is performed at all tolerably.' The *Chromatic Fantasia* is divided into two large sections, the first a constant brilliant swirl of scales and arpeggios, the second a deeply felt recitative-like part, in which a single melody-line wanders off like a vagrant into strange and exotic lands. The fugue begins tranquilly, but erupts in a volcano of energy before the end. The pronounced sense of climax attracts most hearers. There is in the fugue a sense of consummation and completion that can hardly be paralleled. As Forkel wrote: 'I have taken considerable pains to find a similar piece of music by Bach, but without success.'

The nineteen suites for keyboard are divided into six *French Suites* (no introductory movement), six *English Suites* (an introductory prelude), and seven *Partitas* (an introductory movement, variously entitled).

In each of these suites the succession of dance movements follows very much the same pattern: A – C – S – O – G, the dances in order being: *a*llemande, *c*ourante, *s*arabande, an *o*ptional dance, and *g*igue. By way of exception the *B minor Partita* lacks an allemande. The optional dance may be entitled a minuet, a bourrée, a gavotte, a passepied, or even an air. The allemande is cast in moderate $\frac{4}{4}$ time with a quick upbeat at the beginning, the courante in triple time. (At the ends of sections in the courante Bach often momentarily shifts the beat ['hemiola'], so that the last measure or two appears to be in duple instead of triple rhythm.) The third dance, the sarabande, is a slow dance in triple metre, with pronounced emphasis on the second beat. This dance, reputedly of Spanish origin, was described a century earlier as 'a dance so lascivious and so violent in its movements that it is enough to inflame even very respectable people.'

By Bach's time, however, it had lost that particular quality, and in his suites it is almost invariably the tenderest and most expressive number. The gigue, with which his suites ended, is usually in $\frac{6}{8}$ or $\frac{6}{4}$ time; and although not as sprightly as an Irish jig, is always fast and brilliant enough to tax the player's fingers. Every number in a suite is written in the same key[1]; this might prove monotonous were it not that most of the dances last only a minute or two. In each there is a division into two halves with repeat signs at the end of each half.

Of Bach's works for the keyboard the *Goldberg Variations* brought him the greatest financial reward. These *Variations* we owe to Count Kayserling, Russian Ambassador at Dresden, who frequently visited Leipzig with a certain Goldberg, a pupil of Bach's whom he employed. The Count suffered from insomnia; and Goldberg, who lived in the Ambassador's house, slept in an adjoining room so that he could play to Kayserling when he was sleepless. One day the Count asked Bach to write for Goldberg some clavier music of a 'soothing and cheerful' character which would relieve the tedium of sleepless nights. Bach thought a set of variations most likely to meet the Count's needs, although for one reason or another, perhaps because they had the same basic harmony throughout, variations had been a form to which he had hitherto paid little attention.

Like all his compositions of this period the *Variations* are a masterpiece. The Count always called them 'my variations' and was never weary of hearing them. When he could not sleep, Kayserling would say, 'Play me one of my variations, Goldberg.' Certainly Bach was never so well

---

[1] In the *Partita in B Minor* ('French Overture') and in the minor *English Suites* he interpolates dances in the tonic major key.

rewarded for any other composition. The Count gave him a golden goblet containing one hundred *louis d'or*.

The theme that Bach used was a sarabande which he had written in Anna Magdalena's second Notebook (1725) during their early years of married life. The order in which the variations are presented follows a preconceived plan. In the series of thirty variations it runs as follows:

$$F - F - C^1 - F - F - C^2 - F - F - C^3 - F - F - C^4 - F - F - C^5 -$$
$$F - F - C^6 - F - F - C^7 - F - F - C^8 - F - F - C^9 - F - F - Q$$

F in this diagram stands for 'free' variation, C for a canonic variation, and Q at the end for quodlibet.

A quodlibet is a jaunty piece in which two or more popular melodies are played or sung simultaneously. In Bach's quodlibet[1] at the end of the *Goldberg Variations* he introduces two popular tunes, 'I have been away from thee a long while,' and 'Cabbage and turnips'. The amazing ease with which Bach combines the two, and then plays around with them above a predetermined bass is hardly more astounding than the ease with which he constructs his canons. Throughout the entire series the first canon is in unison, the second at the second, the third at the third, and so forth. The voices in the canons always move so as to match precisely the predetermined bass line. At the end of the thirty variations, Bach directed that the original theme be played over again. 'I have shown you all the plants that can be grown from the seeds contained in this little packet,' Bach might have said, 'and now I shall show you the packet again, so that you may realize what innocent-looking seeds were planted in order to grow the garden.'

[1] Other quodlibets occur in the 'Peasant Cantata' and 'Three Wedding Chorals' (incomplete). Forkel said the Bachs at family gatherings took great delight in improvising quodlibets.

The *Goldberg Variations* were conceived for a harpsichord with two manuals. Because the player's hands constantly cross in such variations as 8, 11, 14, 17, 20, 23, 26, and 28, these and others of the thirty are impossible to perform adequately on the modern piano. But under the hands of a skilled harpsichord player such as Wanda Landowska, the *Variations* come to life as one of the most iridescent works in the entire repertory of keyboard music.

Bach's most popular compositions for organ are display pieces in which the performer travels over the keys and pedals at a tremendous rate, builds up huge edifices of sound, and produces dramatic and vivid contrasts in tone colour. The *Toccata and Fugue in D minor* for organ, composed during the Weimar period, begins with several short interjections uttered in the voice of command. Bach proceeds to dazzle the hearer with bright, rapid figures on the manuals, then alternates bold chords with fingery cadenzas, and ends with a fine flourish on the pedals. The Fugue starts with a perpetual-motion subject in which one note, A, alternates with the notes of a descending scale. Its energy never abates, even in subdued passages, and there are unusual opportunities for antiphonal effect at several places.

The different keyboards on organs control the pipes in different parts of the building. Thus in a three-keyboard instrument the lowest manual controls what is called the 'choir' organ — a group of pipes together in one place. The middle manual controls what is called the 'great' organ — a group of pipes elsewhere. And the top manual controls the 'swell' organ — another group somewhere else. Bach exploits to the fullest the separate locations of these various organs, swell, great, and choir, often writing his music in such a way that the organs can answer back and forth. His more popular organ works are by no means rigidly contrapuntal throughout, and they always end with heroic climaxes.

Several of the more brilliant organ works such as the *Prelude and Fugue in D Major*, the *Toccata, Adagio, and Fugue in C Major*, the *Prelude and Fugue in A minor*, and the *Fantasia and Fugue in G minor*, have been transcribed for piano or for full orchestra. For obvious reasons the original organ version may seem less exciting than the transcription. There are fewer concert organists than concert pianists and fewer virtuoso organists than virtuoso orchestras; the standards of performance on the organ today are generally lower than those expected of pianists and orchestras; and only a limited number of first-rate organs exist.

Bach only occasionally based his themes on folk-songs. One instance, we have said, is the quodlibet of the *Goldberg Variations*. Another is the fugue of the *Fantasia and Fugue in G minor* for organ. This work has been connected with Bach's visit to Hamburg in 1720. He was then living at Cothen, but was looking out for a church post and hoped to find it in Hamburg at St. Jacob's Church. On the trial jury was the now ninety-seven-year-old Hamburg organist, Reinken; Reinken had lived in Holland as a youth, and Bach paid him tribute by composing a fugue in which the subject was a favourite Dutch folk-melody. In this work the fantasia contains some of Bach's boldest modulations; in it he seems to ponder deeply the more weighty problems; it is painted in sombre colours. The fugue on the other hand sticks closely to the original key of G minor, and sparkles from beginning to end.

In addition to Preludes and Fugues, Toccatas and Fugues, and Fantasias and Fugues, the catalogue of Bach's organ works contains more than one hundred short pieces of the type called *chorale-preludes*. The singing of chorales (German hymns) was, from the very inception of the Lutheran movement, a central act in public worship. The practice of writing organ pieces in which the chorale tune was ornamented and embellished developed early in Lutheran history. These pieces came to be known as chorale-preludes because they were generally played before the singing of the chorale by the congregation. To understand Bach's compositions of this type, we must imagine a congregation about to sing *Ein' feste Burg* ('A Mighty Fortress is Our God') or *Nun danket alle Gott* ('Now Thank We All Our God'). As an introduction Bach plays an organ piece in which the tune is plainly recognizable. Woven into the melody are rich harmonies, rapid passage-work, or contrapuntal variants, all of which heighten its beauty. Then the congregation sings the chorale tune in unison while the choir adds the other parts that go to make up a full four-part harmony.

Bach's chorale-preludes are among his most easily-enjoyed pieces, even if we do not have the advantage of knowing the tunes beforehand, as his congregations did. The shortest pieces are those in *The Little Organ Book*. There are three other important collections: the so-called 'Catechism' set (*Clavierübung*, Part III, published in 1739), the six Schübler Chorale-Preludes (Schübler was the publisher), and a separate set known simply as 'The Eighteen', because it comprises that number; the two last were compiled during the last four or five years of Bach's life. The Schübler Chorale-Preludes comprise transcriptions for organ of various movements from his own cantatas.

The number of times Bach transcribed his own music gives us adequate justification for transcribing it ourselves today. The problem is not, 'Shall we transcribe Bach?' but rather 'Are our transcriptions faithful to his original intent?' If we answer this last question affirmatively, then we do him no injustice but rather a service in transcribing and even re-naming movements such as 'Jesu, Joy of Man's Desiring', which comes originally from Cantata No. 147 (*Herz und Mund und That und Leben*), or 'Sheep May Safely Graze', from a secular cantata (No. 208, *Was mir behagt*) honouring the birthday of a German princeling, Duke Christian of Weissenfels.

Bach's contributions to every department of musical composition are now considered so important that choirs, organists, harpsichordists, pianists, violinists, and cellists all look to his music as the touchstone of their performing skill. The violinist who can play the six Sonatas for Violin alone, or the cellist who can properly negotiate the six Sonatas for Violoncello alone, has arrived at the *ne plus ultra* of his art as a performer.

The greater part of Bach's orchestral music was composed at Cöthen while he was acting as 'Capellmeister to the excellent Prince of Anhalt-Cöthen'. At his disposal were about fifteen players of such instruments as the violin, viola, cello, bass viol, flute, oboe, bassoon, trumpet, and kettledrums. To this group were added visiting performers, such as two horn players who on June 6, 1722, joined in a performance of the first Brandenburg Concerto in F Major. The six *Brandenburg Concertos*, so named because they were dedicated to the Margrave of Brandenburg (in 1721), are perhaps his most frequently played original works for orchestra.[1]

If we are to single out an identifying trait common to all Bach's concertos it is the element of contrast between a small body of sound and a larger body of sound. This constant alternation is characteristic of the *Italian Concerto* (1735) for harpsichord with two manuals, a solo concerto. The contrast in levels of sound is also found in the concertos for organ solo, in the three concertos for violin with orchestra, the seven for harpsichord with orchestra, the two for two harpsichords with orchestra, and the others for three and even four harpsichords with orchestra; it is also found in the familiar Concerto for Two Violins and Orchestra. The *Brandenburg Concertos* contrast a small group of solo players (differently constituted in each of the six) with the larger body of players who have no solo functions.

The concertos, whatever the instruments used, start as a rule with a fast movement; then comes a slow one; and finally another fast movement. A typical device in the fast movements is the repetition at the end of the same music with which the movement opened. This repetition has the aesthetic appeal of opposite sides in an arched doorway, since it lends symmetry.

An eminent historian of our generation has said that the best way to judge how musical a person is, is to discover his reaction to Bach. Another called Bach the Alpha and Omega of music. All musicians agree that in greatness he is among the first three or four composers of all time.

[1] The Aria from the *Third Orchestral Suite*, especially as transcribed for violin solo ('Air for the G string'), enjoys the distinction of being the most frequently performed single orchestral excerpt, as opposed to any complete work.

Bach's temperament led him to make the great and sublime his goal. For that reason his music is not merely agreeable, like other composers', but transports us to the regions of the ideal. It does not arrest our attention momentarily but grips us the stronger the oftener we listen to it, so that after a thousand hearings its treasures are still unexhausted and yield fresh beauties to excite our wonder.

George Frederick Handel (1685–1759), had he died before his fifty-sixth year, would today be hardly better known than Keiser, Hasse, or Graun, all of whom were his contemporaries and famous during their lifetimes. He owes his popular reputation mainly to his *Messiah*, the oratorio composed in twenty-four days during the late August and early September of 1741. Only one other of his twenty oratorios, *Israel in Egypt*, is still frequently performed. His operas are rarely performed, and never in their original form. A few excerpts from the operas are, it is true, still sung as solos, but even *Ombra mai fù* (popularly known as the 'Largo from *Xerxes*'), though it is so often performed, would hardly be enough to keep his name alive. *The Harmonious Blacksmith*, written for harpsichord, the *Water Music*, a series of short orchestral pieces, mostly dances, and the organ concertos, written originally for organ without pedals, are still played, but any catalogue of Handel's music performed today would be meagre without *Messiah*.

His operas are forgotten because he had no librettist equivalent to Mozart's da Ponte, and because he observed conventions in plot that have passed out of fashion, requiring artificial voices that are no longer available. Except for *Messiah* and *Israel in Egypt*, for which he used Biblical texts, the oratorios have weak and inept eighteenth-century librettos in which Biblical events are so changed about as to make them now seem mere hodge-podges. New characters not found in the Bible are freely invented, often to supply a love-interest. They often have lines assigned to them, moreover, that now seem pompous or inane. *Messiah* is unique, not so much because of its music, but because of its words. It can still be sung without seeming slightly ridiculous, which cannot be said of such oratorios as *Solomon*, with its Queen of Sheba pyrotechnics, or *Joshua*, with its blood-and-thunder heroics, or *Joseph and his Brethren*, with its Egyptian fantasy.

Charles Jennens, compiler of the *Messiah* libretto, also wrote the librettos for *Saul, Belshazzar,* and added *Il Moderato* to *L'Allegro*; his verse is execrable. *Messiah,* whose libretto is a compilation entirely of Scriptural texts, will continue to be the most frequently performed oratorio, and the 'Hallelujah Chorus' the most frequently performed chorus.

Handel's first oratorio, *La Resurrezione*, composed in Rome in 1708, adheres to the traditions of seventeenth-century Italian oratorio. Because any understanding of his achievement as a composer largely depends on a proper understanding of the earlier history of Italian oratorio, a brief synopsis of seventeenth-century oratorio may not be out of place here.

Oratorio is a word which has changed its meaning from time to time over the last four centuries, but the first oratorio, so called, Emilio dei Cavalieri's *La Rappresentazione di anima e di corpo* ('The Representation of Soul and Body') was a mystery play set to music. Produced at Rome in 1600, in the same year as the earliest surviving opera in Florence, it was written to teach a lesson. The characters were abstract personifications such as Pleasure, Intellect, Soul, Body, Time, Life. The characters sang their parts throughout to the accompaniment of a hidden orchestra. They wore costumes and acted on a stage.

The earliest oratorios were 'commissioned' by a group of preachers in Rome, who under the captaincy of St. Philip Neri set about the task of redeeming the outcast. Oratorio was a musical setting of such moral teaching as the Oratorians, as the group was named, wanted them to hear. The oratorio differed from early opera primarily in purpose. Both used costumes and scenery and orchestra and told some sort of story. But the aim of the oratorio was to instruct and edify, whereas that of the opera was to give pleasure.

The most notable oratorio composer of the seventeenth century was Giacomo Carissimi (1605–1674), of whose five oratorios *Jephte* (on the same story as Handel's later work of the same name) is the best known. The words are in Latin, not in Italian, and the text was presumably arranged by Carissimi himself. The time of performance is twenty minutes, about the length of a Bach cantata. (Handel's oratorios, on the other hand, last several hours.) The action in Carissimi's *Jephte* is forwarded by a narrator, called 'Historicus', who in recitative fashion sings the story. This device leaves the soloists, Jephthah and his daughter, free to express pure emotion. They tell no story but merely comment upon it. The chorus, as in a Greek drama, is used to heighten mood, and to repeat what has been sung, but with still greater emotional emphasis and intensity.

Handel discovered the oratorio tradition during his first

Italian visit (1707–1710). He learned not only from models left by Carissimi, but also from the work of Alessandro Scarlatti (1659–1725), who wrote a large number of oratorios as well as innumerable operas. Handel's first oratorio, written the year after his arrival in Italy, demonstrated how completely he had mastered the style of his Italian predecessors. *La Resurrezione* did not, it is true, contain choruses in the manner of his later English oratorios, but in Italy he undoubtedly heard enough oratorios with choral parts to guide him later in his own efforts.

Handel's career reads like the story of a triumphal progress. His father, a barber-surgeon, was sixty-three years old in 1685 when George Frederick was born. His mother was a second wife, the daughter of a Lutheran minister. To her, even after making a great stir in the world, her famous son always returned. He wrote to her constantly, visited her when he could, and never married.

The old father wanted no professional musicians in the family, but a neighbouring duke, the Duke of Weissenfels, heard the child, and persuaded the old man to let him study. An excellent teacher was found, Zachau, thirty-year-old organist of the principal church in Halle, where the Handels lived. Zachau's tuition was a stroke of fortune for the boy, who studied with him for three years. At eleven Handel visited Berlin, then a town of twenty thousand inhabitants, and astounded the court with his skill. He returned to Halle, where his father died soon after. Following his father's wish he enrolled at Halle University, but also held a full-time organ post at the Domkirche, the Calvinist church in the town.

At eighteen he went to Hamburg and secured a post as

violinist in the opera orchestra. He made friends with a brilliant, though erratic, genius, Johann Mattheson; but after a period of close friendship the two fell out. During a run of Mattheson's *Cleopatra* at the Hamburg opera house Handel was assigned the harpsichord. One night Mattheson demanded in an offensive manner that Handel should give up his seat at the instrument. The quarrel ended in fisticuffs. The excited crowd urged the young men to fight a duel. Mattheson later told the story:

> Urged on by others when we left the Opera we came to blows in the public market before a large audience. The duel might have ended very badly for us both, if by God's mercy my sword had not broken in coming into contact with a hard metal button of my opponent's. So no great damage was done.

The quarrel was patched up, but Handel made other enemies. He was so successful in his opera-writing ventures, especially with his first opera, *Almira*, that Keiser, who had ruled the Hamburg operatic roost until Handel arrived, became envious. The young man, soon tired of the pettiness of Hamburg life, set off for Italy. He had no money, but shortly after his arrival there he secured important patrons.

The first notice of him in Rome spoke of him as 'an excellent player' who had succeeded in astounding everyone with his playing on the organ. He performed on the organ of St. John Lateran, and secured a Cardinal, Pietro Ottoboni, one of the wealthiest men in Europe, as a patron. Another wealthy Roman, the Marchese di Ruspoli, commissioned Handel to write his first oratorio. He moved on from Rome to Naples and Venice. At Venice his opera

Agrippina created a sensation. One of the box-holders there was Prince Ernst of Hanover, brother of Georg, later to become George I of England. Prince Ernst, liking the young man's music, invited him to Hanover. At the time of Handel's arrival there the Capellmeister was the gifted Agostino Steffani, priest, composer, and diplomatist. Steffani generously took him under his wing, and introduced him to influential people. Handel later recounted the story: 'When I first arrived in Hanover I was a young man. Steffani received me with great kindness and introduced me to the Princess Sophia, and the Elector's son, giving them to understand that I was a virtuoso in music.'

Steffani suddenly left Hanover, and Handel became Capellmeister at the age of twenty-five. But before he accepted the appointment he asked for leave to visit England. He arrived in London in the autumn of 1710. In late February of the next year he produced his first London opera, *Rinaldo*. Soon after, he returned to Hanover and from there went to Halle to visit his mother. He returned to London in the autumn of 1712. In 1713 Queen Anne gave him an annual pension of £200; the next year she died, but Handel's position improved still further. George arrived in England with a retinue of Germans and became king. Handel, his Hanoverian Capellmeister, the teacher of his children, and the favourite of his wife, shared the good fortune that befell Germans in England at this period. He dominated society with his operatic ventures, and owed no small part of his success to the steady patronage of the royal house. Even when the members of the royal family quarrelled he still held his pension, which George I doubled. George II, who as Prince of Wales had opposed him, added another annual grant of £200 after 1727.

In 1728 a parody on Italian opera, John Gay's *Beggar's Opera*, stole Handel's thunder as well as his box-office receipts. But though he may have lost much money in his impresario ventures, he remained nevertheless personally secure because of his Crown pensions; his own income was never endangered by the perennial crises in the opera business.

He was employed for two years by a notorious war-profiteer, the Duke of Chandos. In his honour Handel wrote twelve anthems, the Chandos Anthems. In 1720 he wrote a 'masque' in six scenes and one act, called *Haman and Mordecai*, with a text by Alexander Pope. For this he is supposed to have received £1,000 of the Duke's doubtfully earned money. Twelve years later this 'masque' was revived in honour of the composer's birthday, and at this revival children from the Chapel Royal sang and costumes with scenery were used. The Princess Anne heard of the 'masque' and wanted a public performance. The Bishop of London, Dr. Gibson, however, frowned on the use of children from the Chapel choir in a public production. He had good reason. *Haman and Mordecai* was in reality another opera, but with a religious subject. In a private presentation the morals of the boys were not subject to the corrupting influence of the professional stage as they would be in a public showing. After the bishop's interdict, Handel enlarged *Haman and Mordecai*, and called it *Esther*. English oratorio, then, may be said to have been born in 1732, when the following announcement appeared in the *Daily Journal* (19 April):

By His Majesty's Command. At the King's Theatre ... will be performed

The Story of Esther

An Oratorio in English. Formerly composed by Mr. Handel, and now revised by him, with several additions, and to be performed by a great number of the best Voices and Instruments.

N.B. — There will be no Action on the Stage, but the House will be fitted up in a decent manner for the Audience. The Musick is so disposed after the manner of the Coronation Service.

Esther, then, was clearly an opera, but on a religious subject and without costumes, scenery, or stage action. Handel would no doubt have presented it with these accoutrements if the Church authorities had not been so strongly opposed to the idea of associating Scripture with the commercial theatre. He is reputed to have made £4,000 from the performances of *Esther* during its first season, which he certainly could not have done if the fashionable public had not been entertained.

The singers in *Esther* included Senesino, the Italian *castrato* who had scored such successes in Handel's earlier operas. Two other Italians, the female stars Strada and Bertolli, also sang. All three Italians are reported to have been very shaky in their English. Senesino again appeared in Handel's second English oratorio, *Deborah*, which was first billed as an opera. The admission fee for *Deborah* was one guinea for a box and half a guinea in the gallery. Though Handel was himself paying Senesino and his other vocalists high fees, these admission prices were considered exorbitant and were greatly resented.

During the 1730's Handel wrote Italian operas and English oratorios alternately. His last opera was produced in the same year that he wrote *Messiah*, which was first performed in Dublin in April 1742. Dublin at that period was an intellectual centre: the great Jonathan Swift, though a sick man, was still Dean of St. Patrick's. Handel never had more enthusiastic audiences than during his nine months in Ireland. The first performance of *Messiah* was an immediate success. To crowd more people into the hall, gentlemen were requested not to wear their swords and ladies were asked to come without their hoops. There were seven hundred present. The following day *Faulkner's Journal* reported: 'Words are wanting to express the exquisite Delight it afforded to the admiring crowded Audience.'

The most outstanding singer in this performance was Susanna Cibber, originally an actress. When she sang the exquisite contralto aria from Part II of *Messiah* in which are described the Saviour's sufferings, 'He was Despised and Rejected of Men, a Man of Sorrows and Acquainted with Grief,' she created a sensation. A clergyman in the audience who knew the sordid details of her past rose to his feet after she had finished the aria and exclaimed: 'Woman! for this thy sins be forgiven thee.'

The first performance of *Messiah* was given for charities. Over £380 was realized. When, on his return to London, Handel tried to present *Messiah* there, Church feeling was so strong against it that he was forced to change its name to *A Sacred Oratorio*. His 'religious farces' on Old Testament themes were resented by the clergy and an entertainment constructed on the life and death of Christ was considered even more scandalous. That *Messiah* was considered 'entertainment' by both Handel and by Jennens is amply proved by their own testimonies. Jennens wrote a letter in which he said: 'Handel has made a fine Entertainment of it, tho' not near so good as he might and ought to have done. I have with great difficulty made him correct some of the grossest faults in the composition, but he retained the overture obstinately, in which there are some passages far unworthy of Handel, but much more unworthy of *Messiah*.' As regards Handel, the evidence is in a remark of his to Lord Kinnoul, in which he thanked him for his praise of the work and added that he hoped not only to have entertained but also to have edified the audience. *Messiah* under its new title was not as great a success in London as it had been in Dublin. In time, however, it grew popular. During his last years Handel produced it annually as a benefit for the London Foundling Hospital.

Handel's oratorios fall into groups. The first three were devoted to Old Testament female characters, *Esther*, *Deborah*, and *Athaliah*. Then came *Saul* and *Israel in Egypt*, both first produced in 1739 with little success. *Messiah* followed; immediately after *Messiah* he began work on *Samson*. There followed several more Old Testament oratorios, including the ill-fated *Joseph*, the prolix *Belshazzar*, and the *pot-pourri* of Psalms called *The Occasional Oratorio*; Handel then wrote a trilogy of three oratorios designed to flatter Jewish national sensibilities, *Judas Maccabaeus*, *Alexander Balus*, and *Joshua*. The attendance at the first of these three was excellent, but the reception of the second and third was not so kind. *Susanna*, one of his great creations, followed in 1749. *Solomon* was produced in the same year. *Theodora*, his only oratorio with a Christian subject other than *Messiah*, appeared in 1750. In 1751 he wrote his last oratorio, *Jephtha*, just before going blind.

Messiah is divided into three parts. The first is concerned with the prophecies of the coming of Christ; the second with the sufferings and death; the third with the resurrection. The oratorio is now most frequently performed at Christmas-time, when church choirs, in order to shorten the work, customarily omit most of Part II and all Part III. The famous 'Hallelujah Chorus' occurs in Handel's score at the end of Part II. Since it gives an effect of finality it can simply be lifted out of its proper place in the scheme and tacked on to a group of excerpts from Part I. The oratorios of Handel were all originally given as Lenten entertainments; the popularity of *Messiah* at Christmas is another of those strange reversals that occur in music history.

It has often been called an 'epic' oratorio, whereas *Esther, Deborah, Athaliah, Samson, Belshazzar, Solomon, Susanna, Theodora,* and *Jephtha,* have been called 'dramatic' oratorios. This is a proper distinction to make. *Messiah* does not attempt to tell a story. Rather it presents a series of terse statements concerning the Messiah, Jesus Christ, upon which chorus and soloists reflect. No one stands and sings a story in recitative fashion. The work seems almost super-personal. The name Jesus, for instance, appears only once in the entire series of fifty-three numbers that go to make up the work (in No. 51). The story of Jesus's life is not its theme. Jennens's compilation of texts concerned itself primarily with the *mission* of Christ, the Anointed One, as revealed in Old Testament prophecy; Isaiah is the source of more of his texts than any other book in the Bible.

The music of *Messiah*, unlike that of *Israel in Egypt* and certain other oratorios, is Handel's own throughout. In *Israel in Egypt* we occasionally encounter choruses which are arrangements from the works of other composers. These show the composer's interest in Italian music, since his indebtedness for the originals can almost always be traced to Italian rather than to German sources. But in *Messiah* he did not borrow, except from his own works. He rearranged certain numbers (7, 12, and 21, for example) from earlier compositions of his own which he had originally conceived with Italian texts.

Unlike Bach, Handel never used chorales in his oratorios. Bach's *Christmas Oratorio* can almost be said to be a succession of chorales, arranged for chorus and orchestra, with interspersed instrumental and solo portions, so frequently do chorales appear. But Handel did not see fit to use them; he, after all, was writing for the English, who could not be expected to know German hymns.

The English influence on Handel can be traced in yet other ways. During the eighteenth century not a few Englishmen thought themselves divinely commissioned to uphold certain religious tenets. Therefore Handel's frequent glorification of the chosen people in his oratorios was regarded by some contemporary Englishmen as a tribute to themselves. His oratorios reflected pride, both in their texts and in their music. Very little anguished soul-searching occurs in the music. The mood expressed in the words, 'God be merciful to me, a sinner,' occurs frequently in Bach's Passions and cantatas. It rarely occurs in Handel's oratorios. His most characteristic mood was 'Hallelujah, the Lord God Omnipotent Reigneth.'

Beethoven gave Handel pride of place among the world's composers. Mozart honoured him and increased the popularity of *Messiah* by adding instruments to its full orchestral score. Haydn reverenced him and, as we have said, was influenced by him when he wrote *The Creation*. Handel may have lost favour in recent years, but in Britain, at leas t, his reputation still stands high. Because of recurring fashions in music, it seems reasonable to suppose that his work — though it may never again be as popular as it was in early nineteenth-century England — may yet rise from the oblivion into which most of it has now unjustly fallen.

Supplementary Readings

Hans T. David and Arthur Mendel have co-operated in issuing *The Bach Reader*, which contains source material for a study of Bach's career.

Philipp Spitta's *Life of Bach*, first published in German in 1873–80, and later translated into English, is still valuable.

Albert Schweitzer's *J. S. Bach* in two volumes has been translated into English, but the original is worth consulting.

C. S. Terry's *Bach: A Biography* is excellent. He has written a number of other useful studies of specialized aspects such as *Bach's Orchestra, Bach's Chorals, Bach: The Historical Approach*. Terry's edition of J. N. Forkel's *Life of Bach* is also useful.

Sir Newman Flower in his biography, *George Frideric Handel*, gave a genial and entertaining account of Handel's life. The second edition (1948) should be used rather than the first.

R. M. Myers wrote illuminatingly on the early history of Handel's most popular oratorio in his book, originally conceived as a Ph.D. dissertation, *Handel's Messiah*.

William C. Smith's *Concerning Handel* and Percy M. Young's *Handel* are both of fundamental value.

The essays assembled by Gerald Abraham in *Handel: A Symposium* contain material of unequal value; but those by Dr. Young and Professor Dent are indispensable.

Additional Supplementary Readings

Chapter I

The New Oxford History of Music, Vol. I, edited by Egon Wellesz, contains authoritatively written chapters on ancient Mesopotamian and Egyptian music (H. G. Farmer, pp. 228–282), Biblical music (C. H. Kraeling, pp. 283–312), Greek music (Isobel Henderson, pp. 336–403), and Roman music (J. E. Scott, pp. 404–420).

Chapter V

Cuthbert Girdlestone's *Jean-Philippe Rameau*.

Chapter VII

Karl Geiringer's *The Bach Family* contains a series of superb essays on J. S. Bach's life and art at pp. 119–295.

A. E. F. Dickinson's *Bach's Fugal Works* provides succinct but useful introductions to his choral as well as keyboard fugues.

Otto Erich Deutsch's *Handel: A Documentary Biography* contains over 800 pages of source-material, most of it having to do with Handel's career in England.

J. P. Larsen in *Handel's Messiah* deals definitively with the origins, composition, and sources of his most popular oratorio.

APPENDIX OF MUSICAL EXAMPLES

Open-score transcriptions of our examples numbered 4–5, 7–10, 12, and 14–17 may be seen in the following recommended sources: (4) Guillaume de Machaut, *Opera*, I (Rome, 1949), pp. 1–6; (5) *Denkmäler der Tonkunst in Österreich*, VII. Jahrgang, pp. 167–8; (7) Ockeghem, *Sämtliche Werke*, Erster Band (1927), ed. D. Plamenac, pp. 99–100; (8) *Werken van Josquin Des Prés*, Wereldlijke Werken, Bundel III (1925), ed. A. Smijers, p. 63; (9) *Denkmäler der Tonkunst in Österreich*, XIV. Jahrgang (1907), p. 15; (10) *Smith College Music Archives*, V, ed. E. B. Helm, pp. 23–4; (12) Palestrina, *Werke*, XXVII, ed. F. X. Haberl, pp. 14–15; (14) *Publikationen Aelterer Praktischer und Theoretischer Musikwerke*, XV. Band, ed. F. Zelle; (15) Monteverdi, *Tutte le opere*, XI, ed. G. F. Malipiero; (16) *Tutte le opere*, VI; (17) *The English Madrigal School*, V, ed. E. H. Fellowes.

Examples 1–3 have been transcribed according to Solesmes rhythmical principles. The tenth and eleventh notes in ex. 2 (bracketed) do not occur in the older MSS., but are found in the Trent Codex from which the Dufay polyphonic setting, ex. 5, was transcribed. In ex. 21 Bach places the older, more primitive version of ex. 2 first in his top part (measures 1–8), and next in his bass (measures 13–26). The plainsong of ex. 1 is transformed by Machaut into an isorhythmic tenor in ex. 4, and by Frescobaldi in ex. 18 into strands which are treated imitatively in all voice-parts.

The words of the *L'homme armé* folksong (ex. 6) were first discovered by D. Plamenac in 1925, and werere published by him in the *Zeitschrift für Musikwissenschaft*, XI (1928–9), at pp. 380–1 ('Miszellen'). Ockeghem's tenor (ex. 7) duplicates the notes of ex. 6 and even the rhythm of the folksong, the only difference which he makes being the insertion of rests between incises.

Mass for Double Feasts I
(Cunctipotens Genitor Deus)

Kyrie eleison

Mode I   10th century plainsong

Ky-ri - e   e -   - le - i - son.
[repeated 3 times]

Chri-ste   e -   le - i - son.
[repeated 3 times]

Ky - ri - e   e -   le - i - son.
[repeated twice]

Ky - ri - e   e -   le - i - son.

Veni Creator Spiritus
Pentecost Hymn

Mode VIII

1. Ve - ni, Cre - a - tor   Spi - ri -   tus,   Men-tes tu - o - rum   vi - si - ta:
2. Qui Pa - ra - cli - tus   di - ce -   ris,   Do-num De - i   al - tis - si - mi,
[five more stanzas follow]

Im - ple su - per - na gra-ti - a,   Quae tu cre - a - sti   pe - cto - ra.
Fons vi - vus, i - gnis, ca - ri - tas,   Et spi - ri - ta - lis   un - cti - o.

Dies irae
Requiem Sequence

Modes I and II, mixed

1. Di - es   i - rae, di - es   il - la,   Sol- vet   sae - clum in   fa - vil - la:
2. Quan-tus tre - mor est   fu - tu - rus,   Quan-do   ju - dex est ven-tu - rus,
7. Quid sum mi - ser tunc di - ctu - rus?   Quem pa -   tro - num   ro - ga - tu - rus?
8. Rex tre-men-dae ma - je - sta - tis,   Qui sal -   van - dos   sal - vas gra - tis,
13. Qui Ma - ri - am ab - sol - vi - sti,   Et la -   tro - nem ex - au - di - sti,
14. Pre - ces me - ae non sunt di - gnae: Sed tu   bo - nus fac be - ni - gne,

Tes-te   Da-vid cum Si-byl-la.   3. Tu-ba mi-rum   spar-gens so-
Cun-cta stri-cte dis-cus-su-rus! 4. Mors stu-pe-bit   et   na-tu-
Cum vix ju-stus sit se-cu-rus. 9. Re-cor-da-re   Je - su pi-
Sal-va   me, fons pi-e-ta-tis. 10. Quae-rens me, se - di - sti las-
Mi - hi quo-que spem de-di-sti. 15. In-ter o-ves   lo - cum prae-
Ne per-en-ni cre-mer i-gne.   16. Con-fu-ta-tis   ma-le-di-

-num   Per se-pul-chra re-gi-o-num, Co-get o - mnes an-
-ra,   Cum re-sur-get cre-a-tu-ra, Ju-di-can - ti res-
-e,   Quod sum cau-sa tu-ae vi-ae: Ne me per - das il-
-sus: Red-e-mi-sti cru-cem pas-sus: Tan-tus la - bor non
-sta, Et ab hae-dis me se-que-stra, Sta-tu-ens in par-
-ctis, Flam-mis a-cri-bus ad-di-ctis: Vo-ca me cum be-

-te thro-num. 5. Li-ber scri-ptus pro-fe-re-tur, In quo to-
-pon-su-ra. 6. Ju-dex er-go cum se-de-bit, Quid-quid la-
-la di-e.   11. Ju-ste ju-dex ul-ti-o-nis, Do-num fac
sit cas-sus. 12. In-ge-mi-sco, tam-quam re-us: Cul-pa ru-
-te dex-tra. 17. O-ro sup-plex et ac-cli-nis, Cor con-tri-
-ne-di-ctis.

-tum con-ti-ne-tur, Un-de mun-dus ju-di-ce-tur.
-tet ap-pa-re-bit: Nil in-ul-tum re-ma-ne-bit.
re-mis-si-o-nis,   An-te di-em ra-ti-o-nis.
-bet vul-tus me-us: Sup-pli-can-ti par-ce De-us.
-tum qua-si ci-nis: Ge-re cu-ram me-i fi-nis.

18. La-cri-mo-sa di-es il-la Qua re-sur-get ex

fa-vil-la Ju-di-can-dus ho - mo re-us

Hu-ic er-go par - ce De-us. 19. Pi-e Je-su Do-mi-

-ne, do-na e-is re-qui-em. A - men.

Messe de Nostre-Dame

Paris: Bibliothèque Nationale, MS *frg. 1584*

Guillaume de Machaut
(1300?-1377)

Kyrie eleison

Veni Creator Spiritus

Florence: Bibl. Naz. Cent., *Magl. XIX 112 bis*

Guillaume Dufay
(1400?-1474)

L'homme armé

Mille regretz

L'Vnzieme livre, contenant Vingt et Neuf Chansons
(Antwerp: T. Susato, 1549)

Josquin des Prez
(1450?-1521)

Isbruck, ich muss dich lassen

Ein ausszug guter alter vnd newer Teutscher liedlein, ed.
G. Forster (Nuremberg, 1539)

Heinrich Isaac
(1450?-1517)

◆ in original =
♭ in transcription

Nous voyons que les hommes

Tiers Livre de Chansons, Nouvellement
Mise en Musique à quatre parties
(Paris: Le Roy & Ballard, 1554)

Jacques Arcadelt
(1504?-1567?)

[other stanzas follow]

Psalme 2. The third Tune

The whole Psalter translated into
English Metre ("Parker's Psalter")
(London: John Day [1567]), fols. XX 2v.-3

Thomas Tallis
(1505?-1585)

\#The Tenor of these partes be for the people when they will syng alone, the other parts, put
for greater queers [choirs], or to suche as will syng or play them priuately (fol. VV4).

Magnificat Tertii Toni

Magnificat Octo Tonum. Liber Primus
(Rome: Alessandro Gardano, 1591)

G. P. da Palestrina
(1525?-1594)

Gloria Patri

Callino Casturame

The Fitzwilliam Virginal Book, No. 158

William Byrd
(1543-1623)

*execution as an "inverted mordent" recommended

Mein G'müth ist mir verwirret

Lustgarten Neuer Teutscher Gesäng
(Nuremberg: Paul Kauffmann, 1601)

.Hans Leo Hassler
(1564-1612)

Mein   Gmüth ist mir ver-wir- ret, das macht ein Jungk- frau zart, bin
gantz vnd gar ver- ir - ret, mein Hertz das kränckt sich

hart,   hab tag vnd nacht kein ruh, führ all - zeit gro-sse klag,

thu stets seuff-tzen vnd wei-nen, in trau-ren schier ver-zag   -zag.

[*four more stanzas follow*]

Lamento d'Arianna

(Venice: Bartolomeo Magni, 1623)

Claudio Monteverdi
(1567-1643)

Part 1

ARIANNA

La - scia - te-mi mo - ri - re   la-scia-te-mi   mo-

-ri - re   e chi vo - le - te voi   che mi con - for - te

* inner parts added

in co-sì du-ra sor-te in co-sì gran mar-ti-re la-

-scia-te-mi mo-ri-re la-scia-te-mi mo-ri-re.

Lamento d'Arianna

Il sesto libro de madrigali a cinque voci
(Venice: R. Amadino, 1614)

Claudio Monteverdi

Part 1

Canto — La-scia-te-mi mo-ri-re, la-

Quinto — La-scia-te-mi mo-ri-re,

Alto — La-scia-te-mi,

Tenore — La-scia-te-

Basso — La-scia-te-mi mo-ri-re, la-

C — -scia-te-mi mo-ri-re

Q — lascia-te-mi mo-ri-re

A — lascia-te-mi mo-ri-re

T — -mi, la-scia-te-mi mo-ri-re e chi vo-

B — -scia-te-mi mo-ri-re

The silver swan
Madrigal

The First Set of Madrigals and Motetts of 5. parts: apt for Viols and Voyces
(London: T. Snodham, 1612)

Orlando Gibbons
(1583-1625)

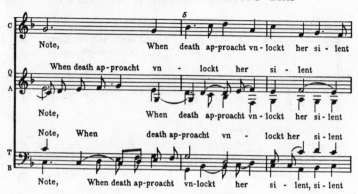

Kyrie delli Apostoli
for Organ

Fiori musicali
(Venice: Alessandro Vincenti, 1635)

Girolamo Frescobaldi
(1583-1643)

When I am laid in Earth
Recitative and Song

Dido and Aeneas, Act III (nos. 36 and 37)

Henry Purcell
(1659?-1695)

*inner parts added in the Recitative

Les Sauvages
for Harpsichord

Pièces de Clavecin [2nd Book]
(Paris, 1724)

J.-P. Rameau
(1683-1764)

Komm, Gott, Schöpfer, heiliger Geist
in Organo pleno con Pedale obligato
Chorale - prelude

Achtzehn Choräle von
verschiedener Art ...
verfertiget (c. 1747)

J. S. Bach
(1685-1750)

Angels, ever bright and fair

Theodora [1750], Act I, Scene 5

G. F. Handel
(1685-1759)

INDEX

Where several page-references follow an indexed item, the one in italics is the principal reference. As a general rule, place-names have not been indexed. Dates have been given in the Index only when not supplied in the main body of the text.